CONCILIUM

concilium 1990/5

COPING WITH FAILURE

Edited by
Norbert Greinacher and
Norbert Mette

SCM Press · London
Trinity Press International · Philadelphia

October 1990

ISBN: 0334 03004 8

Typeset at The Spartan Press Ltd, Lymington, Hants
Printed by Dotesios Printers Ltd, Trowbridge, Wilts

Concilium: Published February, April, June, August, October, December.

For the best and promptest service, new subscribers should apply as follows:
   US and Canadian subscribers:
Trinity Press International, 3725 Chestnut Street, Philadelphia PA 19104
Fax: 215–387–8805
   UK and other subscribers:
SCM Press, 26–30 Tottenham Road, London N1 4BZ
Fax: 071–249 3776

Existing subscribers should direct any queries about their subscriptions as above.

Subscription rates are as follows:
United States and Canada: $59.95
United Kingdom, Europe, the rest of the world (surface): £34.95
Airmail to countries outside Europe: £44.95

Further copies of this issue and copies of most back issues of *Concilium* are available at $12.95 (US and Canada)/£6.95 rest of the world.

Contents

Editorial

As we come to the end of preparing this issue of *Concilium* on the theme of 'Coping with Failure', we ask ourselves whether its planning has been overtaken by the enormous social and political developments in Central and Eastern Europe, and also in other parts of the world, which were unforeseen when we began. Recently 'failure' still expressed a widespread basic mood, so the question of how to deal with such experiences of inadequacy and lack of success was becoming increasingly urgent. Belief in an unstoppable higher development of the human race – in the form of technological progress, economic development, political reform and cultural modernization – was being increasingly undermined. The other side of this development could no longer be suppressed. It was not only the prophets of doom who cannot be taught anything who warned of the increasing number of crises which would result in universal disaster.

But now all at once it seems as though this basic mood of depression has blown away. The slogan of the present no longer seems to be 'failure' but the optimistic feeling that 'We can do it' – at any rate in broad areas of the northern hemisphere. In fact it is impressive and encouraging to see how the pressure for societies living in peace and with self-determination, which people have maintained despite everything, has suddenly burst through after decades of repression, and how the old authorities could ultimately no longer resist the awareness that 'We are the people', expressed increasingly forcefully, so that they had to surrender their positions. This experience that despite many failures a stubborn tenacity and a refusal to be suppressed can in fact lead to the break-up of repressive power structures – and that this can come about through an explicit refusal to exercise one's own power – has become a great encouragement world-wide.

However, to ask anxiously where things will go from here is more than a cheap justification of the theme of this issue. Despite all the encouragement given by the most recent reforms, there is reason for such a question. Above all Western economic forces are undisguisedly exploiting the favourable opportunity of the moment – 'the failure of Socialism', as they say with Schadenfreude – and seizing the chance to expand into markets which had long been closed to them. This move is being encouraged by politicians who loudly promise a definitive end to all the shortages of the past. But is this what the reformers struggled and held out for – individually or in groups?

There has not been enough time to give those involved in these most recent events a say in this issue. The fact that everything was suddenly turned upside down is probably the reason why a contribution from Czechoslovakia, commissioned and firmly promised, never arrived.

We need to note soberly that once again dreams of another society, not just fixated on prosperity and consumerism, threaten to be overwhelmed by what is actually happening. To set hopes on them seems such an uncertain and above all such a laborious step to take that the majority prefer to adopt those maxims for action, characteristic of modern society and supposedly demonstrated by it, which guarantee progress and success: for example the use of ever more efficient technologies, or the application of rationalized administrative machinery. According to this principle of rationality, failure is a disruptive factor which must be excluded in all circumstances. Accordingly the role of human inadequacy, which is essentially responsible for failure, must be kept as low as possible. All other crises can, by contrast, be mastered by the most perfect and effective use possible of those means which are currently at our disposal or are within the reach of technology. Where these do not prove effective, and where success still fails to come, the individual is held to be responsible. How individuals cope with this is left to them. Failure is marginalized, declared a private matter.

This fails to note two things.

First, cases of individual crises in modern societies are increasing rapidly. More and more people are finding it too much, whether in material or psychological terms, to pursue a standard previously set by society in the sectors of either production or consumerism. They are brought to the point of experiencing an existential void. And in the wake of the predominant tendency towards individualization there are increasingly few traditional social contexts like family, kinship, association and so on to serve as protection. The result is that those affected are increasingly thrown back on themselves. Regardless of the degree to which failure must be understood as an element of the human condition, this indication makes it clear how social changes can have far-reaching effects on the experience of failure, and on copying with it. Even if the promise of a 'brave new world' cannot be fulfilled in principle without failure, that does not mean that no steps can be taken to reduce failure by relevant care and guidance. It is all the more alarming to see an increase here rather than a decline – a clear indication that socially an attitude has come to predominate which is solely concerned with the smooth functioning of the mechanisms which support the system and is therefore ready to put up with risks and crises in the individual sphere.

Secondly, the risks and crises that need to be mentioned have long become systemic, making urgent the question whether the project of modern industrial society has not failed – a failure which threatens to bring with it the annihilation of humankind and the destruction of the world. The historical extent that this threat has meanwhile assumed is impressively demonstrated by the World Assembly on Justice, Peace and the Integrity of the Creation held in Seoul:

> 'Every *minute* the countries of the world spend 1.8 million US dollars on military equipment;
> Every *hour* 1500 children die of hunger or of diseases caused by hunger;
> Every *day* a plant or animal species becomes extinct;
> In the 1980s, every *week* more people were arrested, tortured, put to flight or oppressed in other ways by repressive governments than at any other time in history.
> Every *month*, through the international economy, a further 7.5 billion US dollars are added to the 1500 billion dollar debt which has already put an intolerable burden on people in the Third World;
> Every *year*, the rain forest is irretrievably decimated by a surface area corresponding to two-thirds of Korea;
> Every *decade*, the temperature of the earth's atmosphere will rise drastically (by 1.5 to 4.5 degrees Celsius by the middle of the next century), raising the sea level, if the present global warming continues. This will have devastating effects, above all on the coastal areas of all continents.

For the first time in human history it is possible for human beings completely to destroy their own species and the *oikos*, the house, in which they live. And here already the life-and-death battle for survival on this planet is already having cruel effects. Since the Ecumenical World Assembly in Seoul failed to satisfy the expectations of many Christians, the task of reminding world Christianity of its responsibility in the face of these threats is all the more urgent.

The contribution by Carmen Pérez, written in a country in which this fight for survival has become an oppressive everyday concern for the great majority of the population, reports this reality in a shattering and yet hopeful way. It is at the same time a testimony to the difficulty of really putting the reality of failure into words.

Despite the threatening, indeed already destructive, magnitude which individual and global crises have reached, it is by no means certain that these experiences of failure are being tackled on a wide scale. Rather, they are being brushed aside with the excuse that it is impossible to live permanently face to face with this situation. People withdraw into the private sphere and at least there seek to do the best they can. Some even take pleasure in the thought that it will soon be all up not only with them but with everyone else. Yet others take refuge in a hectic activism. And finally they increasingly cover up with cynicism the failure for which they once stood up and which they cannot deny.

Is there, by contrast, a way of coping with failure and defeat which does not just end up in the suppression of such experiences, in resignation, or in attempts to compensate for them with masochistic strategies? How is it possible not to deny failure, but to live with such experiences in human and Christian terms? These were the main questions during the planning of this book. Experiences of failure in its pathological and creative forms are the theme on which reflections are made.

Two introductory essays sketch out the breadth of the theme, illuminate its background, indicate differences and give first indications of possible ways of coping. The first has a more marked anthropological orientation (Norbert Greinacher), while the second puts more stress on epistemological problems (J. Mark Thomas). Under the title 'Religion as a Praxis for Coping with Contingency', Alois Müller discusses whether and how far religion is to be defined in terms of the expectations attached to it above all in individual and also social boundary situations. He offers an illuminating survey of more recent philosophical positions and questions them. Karl-Josef Kuschel pursues a journey on the theme in yet another direction. He introduces prototypes of failed existence from German post-war literature and shows how these are at the same time to be regarded as seismographs of a society confronted with the experience of failure with which it cannot cope.

The second thematic block discusses experiences of failure and ways of coping with it in a variety of contexts. Dietmar Mieth begins from the experience of those affected and develops an illuminating phenomenology of failure on an individual level which demonstrates the possibilities of a new beginning. Erika Schuchardt has investigated through biographies whether and how far failure goes with the opportunity to learn to lead a new life. Her resultant model of a process of coming to terms takes the form of a spiral.

Finally, in the contribution by Nazaire Bitoto Abeng there is a case-study from the sphere of the church: the situation of the Catholic Church in Africa is significant for the contemporary situation of the Catholic

Church generally, which faces the failure of intention to bring about a fundamental self-renewal, solemnly proclaimed at the Second Vatican Council, solemnly proclaimed, and greatly hoped for by many people. This failure will inevitably have consequences. For an increasing number of people are asking what the promise of final salvation through a God who is love, of which the church is still a vehicle, has to do with a church politics deliberately aimed at the failure of reform which does not even shrink from brutality.

Whether the church lives up to this promise is demonstrated not only in church politics but – indeed, primarily – in the specific way in which it deals with those who encounter it. Here too there is a painful experience that the church not only cannot support people in a situation of failure but indeed makes this situation worse by practices of accusation, debasement and exclusion. The aim of the article by Elisabeth Bleske with which the third thematic block begins is to draw attention to the urgent need of at last making changes here – changes which are also called for by biblical teaching. Here she uses the church's doctrine of marriage as a paradigm to demonstrate the church's inability to guide people through failure with understanding and solidarity.

Jürgen Ebach calls for an even more far-reaching revision of some now common theological conceptions, above all those which seek to keep God remote from all failure, in an interpretative recollection of the biblical Exodus story as a history of failure. Here, paradigmatically, we have a hermeneutic of conflict and crisis which can show critical and innovative power in dealing with failure on a theological basis. It is taken up and developed further in the concluding theological essay by Gotthard Fuchs, 'Does God Fail?'

Finally, reference should be made to an earlier issue of *Concilium*, 169: *Job and the Silence of God*, November 1983. Unfortunately *Concilium* 12.3, 1976, which dealt with the same theme as this issue, was never translated into English.

Norbert Greinacher
Norbert Mette

I · Approaches

The Ambivalence of Failure and Human Ambivalence

Norbert Greinacher

A fourteen-year-old Jewish boy from Galicia who had been put in a concentration camp by the Nazis wrote the following letter:

> Dear parents,
>   Even if heaven were paper and all men ink, I could not describe my grief and all that I see around me. The camp is in a clearing. Early in the morning they drive us into the forest to work. My feet are bleeding because they have taken away my shoes. We work all day with virtually nothing to eat, and at night we sleep on the earth (they have even taken away our coats). Every night drunken soldiers come and hit us with wooden clubs and my body is as black as charcoal from all the bruises. Sometimes they throw us a few raw carrots or a beetroot, and it's awful – here people fight to get a piece or a leaf. The day before yesterday two boys escaped; they put us in a row and every fifth person in the row was shot. I was not the fifth, but I know that I shall not get out of here alive. Goodbye to you all, dear mother, father, brothers and sisters – I weep.[1]

In the face of the cruel example of reality which we call the Holocaust, the notion of Gottfried Wilhelm Leibniz, who in 1697 used the term 'theodicy' for the first time, that this is the best of all possible worlds, seems fearful cynicism. Leibniz writes:

> The unbounded wisdom of the Almighty, together with his immeasurable goodness, has brought it about that, all things seen together, nothing better could come into being than what has been created by God . . . Therefore, whenever something in the works of God seems blameworthy, one has to assume that we do not know it sufficiently,

and that the wise man who could see through it clearly would judge that nothing better could be desired.[2]

So the phrase 'the ambivalence of failure' in the title of this article needs to be protected against misunderstanding. The whole burden of suffering, the cruelty of failure, cannot be forgotten and suppressed. It is trivialization, indeed cynicism, to attempt to balance disconcerting suffering against a possible good that could perhaps come out of it. That happens when someone superficially or even in a bigoted way says, 'All suffering also has its good sides.' So we must attempt to look more closely at what is meant by the ambivalence of failure.

It cannot mean giving a positive interpretation to suffering which transcends those affected, the sufferers. That would be to philosophize or theologize without a subject. The history of each person's suffering must be taken seriously. It is more important to listen to what those who are hurt and beaten themselves say about their suffering than to write about the nature of suffering and sorrow. Nor can there be any question of privatizing and individualizing the injustice and grief that is suffered – a great danger, given the widespread apathy in our society. We have to discover its social causes and publicly accuse particular people and social institutions which cause human suffering.

Above all in the history of Christianity human suffering and failure have been ideologized time and again – sometimes down to the present day. Let me quote one text as an example of a widespread attitude in the church. In the middle of the last century, when ten-year-old children were suffering agonies in the factories of France and thirty-year-olds were being dismissed as old men, a bishop wrote to his diocese, in which the poor made up forty per cent of the population:

> Comfort yourselves with the thought that the divine Saviour wanted to put you in the most happy situation of working for your salvation by giving you a share in his cup of need and deprivation . . . and if you share in these you will share in the crown of glory . . . That he chastizes (even the good) in this world according to his mercy so as not to punish them according to his righteousness in the other.[3]

The classical themes for a religious ideologizing of failure can be described as testing, education and punishment. From this perspective, human suffering and failure are a deliberate punishment from God. Just as parents punish a disobedient child, as the king or the state punishes an evildoer, so God punishes sinful men and women, indeed a sinful people, by failure.

Bound up with this is another conception. Failure is the education of men and women by God. Through suffering and distress human beings mature. God, too, acts in accordance with the saying of the ancient Greeks, 'He who loves his son strikes him.' Out of love for men and women he sends suffering as a test in order in this way to lead people to a deeper faith.

So there is also a 'masochism of the pious'[4] which virtually seeks sorrow, indeed is in love with sorrow and failure. One can also enjoy suffering and create desire from self-hatred. The masochism then quite often turns into sadism: if I enjoy my suffering in self-destruction, why should I not then also make others suffer and involve them in my failure?

But must we not follow Ernst Bloch in calling such a God, who educates through suffering, feels satisfaction at punishment, and indeed requires the bloody sacrifice of his son on the cross to atone for human sin, 'the cannibal in heaven'?[5]

No. Such ambivalence of failure is not meant here. By contrast, Jesus attempted to react to failure in human terms and at the same time also to investigate the causes of failure (cf. John 9). These will always be very varied, and one's own fault and the fault of others will often be interwoven. But perhaps in view of human failure it is meaningful to ask where the causes are primarily to be sought. As a model, perhaps the following considerations may be helpful.

First of all should be mentioned the failure for which we ourselves are primarily responsible: I may the chief cause of the break-up of a marriage, of ruining my health, losing my job, killing another person through an accident. My answer to this failure for which I am responsible will above all consist in mourning individually, i.e. looking in myself for the grounds and causes, changing my inner attitudes and my exterior, and as far as possible making good the damage I have caused.

But it can also be that I am the member of a community – a family, a group, an association, a people – which has become guilty, indeed has failed collectively, without myself being individually guilty of this failure. Nevertheless I must share in bearing responsibility for the consequences, and cannot escape the complex of guilt. Federal President Heuss rightly said that the failure of German National Socialism was not a collective guilt but a collective shame. There is a historical responsibility based on my integration into a particular community.

It is quite another matter if above all other people, social classes, social and economic structures and institutions cause my failure and the failure of my social class and my people. In that case the appropriate reaction can be protest, rebellion, indeed a fight against the failure and its cause.

Different again is the situation when individual or collective failure is brought about by natural catastrophes (here for the moment I leave aside the important fact that to an increasing degree human beings cause, or have a share in causing, natural catastrophes as a result of basically wrong behaviour). Leibniz's trust that God has created the best of all possible worlds, which from our present perspective is highly problematical, was seriously shaken in the consciousness of the European West on 1 November 1755 when Lisbon was reduced to rubble and ashes in a few minutes as the result of an earthquake and about 60,000 people met a terrible fate. P. -W. Gennrich rightly judges: 'At that time the world-view of an age tottered; belief in divine providence and the rationality of the world was given a decisive blow. The optimism of the Enlightenment collapsed.'[6] And people asked themselves the same question about the earthquake in Messina on 28 December 1908, to which more than 100,000 people fell victim. Is it really a Christian answer to say what a preacher said at the time: 'God was also in the earthquake?'[7]

Whatever may be the causes for human failure, the first and basic answer will be an attitude of sympathy, compassion on those affected, even, indeed precisely, if they bear some responsibility for their failure. Failure, in all its forms, may not lead to a passive suffering, to an acceptance of fate, to a dull putting up with it. Failure calls for the solidarity of those who have failed, and also the solidarity of those who have not failed with those who have. What Gustavo Gutiérrez wrote about attitudes to the poor also applies to attitudes to those who have failed: 'Christian poverty, an expression of love, is solidarity with the poor and is a protest against poverty.'[8]

Only against the background of what has been said so far can one speak of a real ambivalence of failure. Without robbing failure in the least of its fearfulness or trivializing this, failure *can* also be an opportunity for those who have failed. Certainly human beings often fall apart under their fate: either literally, in that failure leads to physical and psychological destruction, or in that failure drives those concerned to despair so that they remain broken men and women for the rest of their lives.

But there is also the possibility of experiencing the depths of human life in failure and so maturing. Only those who know despair, says Elie Wiesel, also know life. And Karl Jaspers speaks of fruitful despair.[9]

Much depends on the attitude that we take to setbacks, conflicts, frustrations, defeats, guilt and failure: whether we experience and interpret them as kismet, as some destiny which has been thought up and inflicted on us by someone, or whether we accept them as a challenge: as a possibility of exerting all our physical and psychological powers, as a chance for conversion and a new beginning, as a possibility for maturing, as a field of new experiences and new insights.

It is very easy to write this in a safe place where one is well looked after.

But what if one's experience is like that of the psalmist: 'But I am a worm and no man, scorned by men and despised by the people' (22.7)?

Nevertheless, failure can represent an opportunity for change. If one uses one's strength to draw on the depths of human life, if one succeeds in analysing the causes of failure in oneself and others, this can be the beginning of a change within oneself and of rebellion against inhuman institutions. Failure also offers the possibility of a more human life. If we understand human *learning* as a change in inner attitudes and external modes of behaviour on the basis of new insights and new experiences, then failure can offer the possibility of learning: as an individual, or together with others who are also affected by the same failure.

Seen from this perspective, the ambivalence of human failure points to the fundamental ambivalence of human life generally. In his story *Light*, Christoph Meckel writes: 'What kind of a life is it which is worth living by breaking out of? What kind of conditions make it necessary to break out? Where have we got to? Are we still there? Utter ambivalence.'[10]

Here, too, talk of human ambivalence has to be protected from misunderstanding. That does not mean that even the unchangeably good person can also be threatened, that he or she is also occasionally guilty, but something more basic, something perhaps felt by those Greeks who in 440 BC were gathered in the theatre of Dionysus in Athens and heard that hymn to humankind which Sophocles prefaced to his *Antigone*: 'Much is tremendous, but nothing is more tremendous than man.' In connection with this hymn of Sophocles, Walter Jens writes: 'It has proved to be the most perfect interpretation of the human Janus-face, an interpretation which has yet to be achieved even now by science, philosophy and art, of that hermaphrodite whose greatness is identical with its depth – identical, because the tremendous in the sense of "great, mighty, powerful", and the tremendous which means "uncanny, creepy, threatened and confused" condition one another.'[11]

Is that not also our experience? I remember a day in my life as if it were yesterday. I was visiting the remains of Mydanek concentration camp in Poland. I saw the gas ovens, the mountains of human ash, the collections of clothing and the piles of toys of murdered children. And I felt so wretched, so disgusted with my own humanity, that I could have spat on myself.

Mydanek, Dachau, Auschwitz, and in another way Dresden, Hiroshima, Nagasaki: names, signs of what human beings are capable of, of what monsters they are, of how nameless and boundless is the human suffering that people impose on one another.

Failure is the place where the question of theodicy is raised in the most radical form. Can the omnipotence and goodness and love of God be reconciled with the unspeakable suffering of human beings and their failure? In our historical situation we have not only the question of Theodor W. Adorno whether one may still write poems after Auschwitz,[12] but the more radical question whether in view of the unspeakable misery in the world, of the millionfold hunger and famine, of the inhumanities in this world which cry out to heaven, one can still believe in God, or whether absolute meaninglessness does not have the last word.

Though I cannot go more closely philosophically and theologically into the question of theodicy here,[13] I share the conviction of Immanuel Kant, expressed in his essay 'On the Failure of All Philosophical Attempts at Theodicy',[14] 'that our reason is quite incapable of achieving any insight into the relationship between a world as we can know it through experience and supreme wisdom'.[15] The theologian has virtually nothing to add to that!

But what is to be done in a situation of failure, if reason and revelation cannot give us any ultimately satisfying answer? Previous generations were called on to learn to suffer without complaining. The opposite is the case if one thinks of all the Jewish and Christian traditions. Only those who complain take God and themselves seriously.

Above all the Jewish traditions call on us to express our suffering and not think it blasphemous, but human, to put questions to God.

A friend of Romano Guardini told me that Guardini had said to him on his deathbed. 'I am ready to go before the divine judge and answer his questions about my life. But I shall also have questions to put to the judge. Questions about the suffering of innocent children.'

The rights of human beings before God, the right to ask God to account for himself, to put God on trial, indeed to argue with God, have a long tradition. We may recall the figure of Job in the Old Testament, who cries out to God: 'Do not condemn me; let me know why you contend against me. Does it seem good to you to oppress, to despise the work of your hands and favour the designs of the wicked?' (10.2f.). And we recall above all that question with which, according to the testimony of Matthew, Jesus of Nazareth died, and which is part of Psalm 22, which begins, 'My God, my God, why have you forsaken me, and are far from my crying, the words of my lament? My God, I cry by day but you give no answer; I call by night and find no rest' (22.2f.).

Lamentation and crying to God in a situation of failure is a response worthy of God and human beings. We know of Jesus that at the moment of his failure he acted like this: 'and at the ninth hour Jesus cried with a loud voice' (Matt. 27.46). Elie Wiesel tells us of Rabbi Levi-Yitshak: 'Before the mussaph prayer on Yom Kippur he cried out, "Today is the day of judgment. David proclaims it in his psalms. Today all men stand before you for you to condemn them. But I, Levi-Yitshak, the son of Sarah, from

Berdichev, I say and proclaim that you are the one on whom judgment is passed today. Your children will do it, those who suffer for you, who die for you, to allow your name, your law and your promise to be hallowed.'[16] Wiesel's comment is: 'Whereas other mystics maintained a relationship with God on an interpersonal level, Levi-Yitshak allowed himself to threaten God with the breaking off of these relationships. He loved to demonstrate that one can be a Jew with God, in God and even against God, but not without God.'[17]

Jesus did not seek suffering nor death, but he did not avoid suffering either. However, Jesus was not a masochist in search of suffering. Pain did not give him any pleasure. Jesus' death on the cross is not a justification for human suffering but is in truth the extreme consequence of his fight against suffering. Thomas Pröpper rightly observed: 'And to this degree one may and must also say that we are not really redeemed through and thanks to the death of Jesus but despite this death.'[18]

Romano Guardini once raised the theoretical question: what would have happened had the great majority of the people of Israel accepted Jesus and recognized him as the promised messiah? Would Jesus then perhaps have died as an old man, recognized by all and revered in the weakness of his old age?[19] That is certainly just a flight of fancy, but perhaps it can make one thing clear to us. God does not want human suffering. God certainly does not want the death of his Son, but above all and basically he wants the salvation and happiness of all human beings.

Human failure becomes sharpest in death. Martin Heidegger teaches us that the whole of human life is 'being towards death'. But in dying, in the vestibule of what in human terms is final suffering, the question is raised once again in a radical way: is there or is there not an all-embracing transcendent reality which gives meaning to my life and death?

I met Ernst Bloch some time before his death. He was smoking his pipe with enjoyment; he refilled it and said: 'Death is exciting. Will there be something? Will there be nothing? Will there be tobacco?'

Even for believers, there is a dialectical attitude in their hour of failure, as the death of Jesus shows. According to the testimony of Matthew, Jesus cried out, 'My God, my God, why have you forsaken me?' (27.45). According to Luke, he cried out, 'Father, into your hands I commend my spirit' (23.46). Whatever the reality may have been, these differing reports show how differently human beings deal with failure, how ambivalent is human failure, how ambivalent is human life and death.

Translated by John Bowden

Notes

1. *Letzte Briefe zum Tod Verurteilter aus dem europäischen Widerstand*, Munich 1962.

2. G. W. Leibniz, *Die Sache Gottes verteidigt durch die Versöhnung seiner Gerechtigkeit mit seinen übrigen Vollkommenheiten und mit all seinen Handlungen*, 46–48.

3. Quoted from M. Legree, 'Die Sprache der Ordnung', *Concilium* 12, 1976, 555.

4. Cf. T. Pröpper, 'Warum gerade ich? Zur Frage nach dem Sinn von Leiden', *Katechetische Blätter* 13, 1983, 253–74.

5. E. Bloch, *Atheismus im Christentum*, Reinbek 1970, 160.

6. P. -W. Gennrich, 'Gott im Erdbeben, Naturkatastrophen und die Gottesfrage. Eine geistes- und theologiegeschichtliche Studie', *Pastoraltheologie* 65, 1976, 343–60:343.

7. Ibid., 351.

8. G. Gutiérrez, *A Theology of Liberation*, Maryknoll and London 1973, 172.

9. Quoted from R. Boschert, 'Krise und Existenz. Von den Aufgaben des Sozialpädagogen in der Krisenbegleitung', *Neue Praxis* 17, 1987, 326–35:328.

10. C. Meckel, *Licht*, Munich 1978, 70.

11. W. Jens, *Kanzel und Katheder*, Munich 1984, 69.

12. T. W. Adorno, *Negative Dialectics*, London 1973, pp. 362f.

13. From recent times see esp. G. Gerstenberg and W. Schrade, *Leiden*, Stuttgart 1977; G. Greshake, 'Leiden und Gottesfrage', *Geist und Leben* 50, 1977, 102–21; H. Küng, *Gott und das Leid*, Einsiedeln ⁷1980 D. Sölle, *Suffering*, London 1976; E. Schillebeeckx, *Christ*, New York and London 1980, 670–723: 'Leiden und christlicher Glaube', *Concilium* 12, 1976.

14. I. Kant, *Werke* (10 volumes), ed. W. Weischedel, Darmstadt 1983, Vol. 9, 105–24.

15. Ibid., 114.

16. E. Wiesel, *Chassidische Feier*, Vienna 1974, p. 106.

17. Ibid., 104f.

18. Pröpper, 'Warum gerade ich?' (n. 4), 270.

19. R. Guardini, *The Lord*, London 1956, 153–8.

Does Humanity Fail in What it Knows?

J. Mark Thomas

A full-page advertisement for the Lockheed Corporation in the 31 October 1989 issue of the *Wall Street Journal* is an exegesis of the relationship between 'The Tower of Babel and Systems Integration'. Peter Brueghel the Elder's painting of the Tower (ca. 1560) occupies fully the lower two-thirds of the page. Even in newspaper reproduction, the proud ziggurat he paints manifests itself as the centre of ferocious activity. It is portrayed as a building hewn from raw stone, the object of the movements of boats and transports coming and going. Workers and artisans scurry over every part of the edifice, and in the lower right-hand corner they pay due homage to the ruler, his ministers and his military escort – the powers and the principalities. The massive structure reaches into the clouds, even while sections of each of its many floors remain under construction, revealing the detailed innards of its form. Earthly power in all of its technical brilliance is here, towering over the village and countryside which spread in panorama in the background. And above this sixteenth-century visual interpretation of the biblical story, the Lockheed Corporation adds an analysis of its own.

The beginning of this exegesis is surprisingly orthodox. It says that the parable of the Tower of Babel (Genesis 11) concerns the activity of a people on the plain of Shinar who attempted to build an 'altar to their own intellect', and because they all 'spoke one common language . . . nothing was impossible to them'. When God saw what they were doing, however, the 'hubris of this arrogant race angered him', so God cursed the city with hundreds of languages, bringing confusion and impotence.

The interpretation then seeks to draw its homily from the parable. The lesson of the tower is 'remarkably prescient for us in the twentieth century', writes the unknown advertising copywriter. The past four decades of computer development has brought with it the 'ancient curse of Babel', because the proliferation of computer companies has brought simultaneously the use of different formats and languages. Thus, there is confusion, just like that created in Babel.

> Recognizing this discord, Lockheed has a solution: systems integration. For years the company has been synthesizing apparently incompatible systems, whether for use in space, the military, or private industry. To this end, Lockheed has actually been able to work against the Babel effect. And with everyone once again speaking the same language, who knows what wonders are possible?

Thus ends the lesson. The modern meaning of the parable is that twentieth-century persons must engineer a solution to the problem of the fragmentation of knowledge which the residents of the plain of Shinar could not do. Incoherence is an instrumental problem that can be fixed by the same technologies that build towers. Whether applied to 'space, the military, or private industry', humanity fails in what it knows in so far as it allows disparate information technologies to prevent a unified data system capable of reversing the 'Babel effect'. This can be accomplished by the very 'systems integration' offered by the Lockheed corporation.

What would this solution mean? Knowledge would be made what it can be. This contemporary technological soteriology ostensibly parallels the biblical drama of salvation: an original creation marred by the fall, and redeemed *a fortiori* in the kingdom of God. Lockheed's exegesis suggests a movement from the origins wherein a people united in language found that 'nothing was impossible to them', to the fallen, post-Babel condition wherein '[n]othing was possible', to the return to the original condition wherein 'wonders are possible'. The technological kingdom is one in which the original limitless capacity of humanity – lost in diffuse information – is restored and enhanced. That in reality the original condition portrayed could never have achieved the unity of knowledge possible in an integrated computer system makes the exegesis not only perverse, but disingenuous.

For modernity, however, this odd advertisement undoubtedly manifests the hegemonic answer to the question, 'Does humanity fail in what it knows?' It fails only insofar as it does not achieve the perfection of the technical system that has been put into place. As the popular scientific magazine, *Omni*, once quipped, 'The meek shall inherit the earth. The rest of us will go to the stars!' Cognitive unity is accompanied by technological progress, and the two form the soteriological core of the contemporary era.

What is significant in this advertisement is not that a major American corporation will use a biblical story to sell products, nor even that the use of the story contradicts its traditional interpretation. It is, rather, that this commercial demonstrates paradigmatically the primary way in which contemporary humanity fails in what it knows: it does not grasp the ambiguity pervading its own knowing.

Before this claim can be elaborated, however, some qualifications concerning the question itself must be made.

Does humanity fail in what it knows? Who is included in this 'humanity' about which the question is asked? What counts as knowledge, and, significantly, what constitutes the failure to know? The obvious enormity of the question is that it embraces the heart of epistemological and anthropological inquiries. In lieu of a sustained treatment of both of these dimensions, therefore, some clarifications should be made to indicate what it meant by each term.

For the purposes of this conversation, 'humanity' is taken to mean a reality both of historical and ontological significance. There is something distinct about 'being human' itself, and it is that distinction which is appealed to in the question under consideration. 'Humanity' refers to the self-consciousness of persons rather than that of other creatures, or of God. And most significantly, this self-consciousness is reflexive, questioning not only the world in its totality, but the very consciousness by which it questions.

Further, as 'finite freedom' (Paul Tillich), humanity also participates in the vicissitudes of historical reality. This reality is itself fragmented and pluralistic, to be sure, but it apparently sustains dominant or hegemonic actualities over time. With some reason, one era is spoken of as 'medieval' and another as 'industrial'. One society is spoken of as 'tribal' and another as 'bureaucratic'. Thus, to speak of the self-consciousness that determines contemporary reality as technical reason is to recognize its hegemony rather than to assign it absolute status. Still, in so far as it now reaches into all segments of the world, it is increasingly difficult to speak of 'pluralism' as one might have done only fifty years ago. It is technical reason and the challenges to it that dominate the intellectual landscape of modernity.

Humanity fails in what it knows, in so far as it does not grasp the ambiguity of knowing. Bernard Lonergan's analysis certainly leads in this direction. If the failure to understand humanity and its condition 'dialectically' represents for him the chief reason for historical decline, the consequences are no less dialectical than the cause:

So we are brought to the profound disillusionment of modern man and to the focal point of his horror. He had hoped through knowledge to ensure a development that was always progress and never decline. He has discovered that the advance of human knowledge is ambivalent, that it places in man's hands stupendous power without necessarily adding proportionate wisdom and virtue, that the fact of advance and the evidence of power are not guarantees of truth, that myth is the permanent alternative to mystery and mystery is what his hubris rejected.[1]

What Lonergan here calls 'ambivalent' may be better called 'ambiguous', in so far as the progress of human knowledge has resulted not merely in psychological anomie, but in obvious forms of social destruction. Even the information revolution to which the Lockheed advertisement refers allows for both the centralization of cancer research, and the mapping of the earth for the targeting of 'smart' missiles. Rapid information-gathering and processing makes possible the co-ordination of large enterprises, such as a hospital, or a covert agency keeping track of political dissidents. Biological advances promise new weapons in the arsenal against disease. But they also feed new arsenals for warfare, and as the economist Herman Daly has noted, through bio-engineering they seek to substitute market mechanisms for evolutionary wisdom in the distribution of biological life. The flight from intelligence which Lonergan identifies represents the moral and intellectual ambiguity of knowledge. The 'surd' is wedded to intelligence, and only transcendent power can overcome the destructiveness of this mixture.

Humanity fails in what it knows in so far as it tries to escape ambiguity by destroying the polar character of knowledge. If in the cognitive realm the perennial problem of epistemology is the relation between the subject and the object, knower and known, the mark of the Fall is that knowing is resolved either into the subject or the object. In this way, the polarities of being (necessary for the process of life) are fractured into antitheses (destructive of being). The self is cut off from the world, either by collapsing the world into the self, or losing the self in the world. One way of knowing places its entire intellectual wager on the 'objective' character of what is to be known, the 'out there' of reality, and will thus attempt to remove the knower from the act of knowing. 'Objectivism', in its many forms, seeks such knowledge. And to the degree that reality meets human consciousness in this way, objectivism is successful in what it knows. The dispassionate inquiry into inorganic matter, for instance, seems not only possible but fitting in a fundamental way. And yet, even physics has suspected for some time through the work of the quantum theorists of the Copenhagen school that the participation of the observer in what is being observed changes the reality. Competing epistemologies will wager on the involved, living, experiential character of knowing, and thus 'subjectivism' in one of its variants will come to the fore. While earlier in the century existentialism, vitalism and phenomenology moved in this direction, now elements of feminist, critical, and literary theory take up the cause. A third option – always present but never dominant – is the way of mystical union, attempting to transcend in consciousness both subject and object in order to reunite with Being as such. Much of the Romantic movement (historical and contemporary) strives for such cognition. This may be sought in a transcendent manner, as in asceticism, or in an immanental way, as in some forms of existentialism. In either case, however, the ontological tension between subject and object is relieved by the annihilation of the polarities themselves.

Humanity fails in what it knows by shattering the living polarities in which vibrant life takes place, and it generally copes with this failure by taking refuge under the wing of subject or object, self or world. The 'coincidence of opposites' noted since the time of Heraclitus becomes a choice between antitheses. Why is there such a general ontological failure? As Eric Fromm described the 'flight from freedom' in his search for understanding of the Fascist phenomenon, perhaps the 'flight from ambiguity' must now be understood. Living with cognitive and practical ambiguity requires intellectual and moral courage. It demands the cognitive element of what Paul Tillich called the 'courage to be'. As such, it is an act of faith. This faith can live with ambiguity because it rests upon a reality that transcends, unites and grounds both subject and object. It gives the courage to live with the world as it is – wheat and weeds together – because it does not derive ultimacy from either subject or object. And yet, it is impossible merely to summon such courage, or to structure it intentionally into a human community. Rather, such courage grasps and shakes some persons and some communities at some points in human history, unpredictably, if not mysteriously. For example, it must have been a form of intellectual courage that grasped Martin Luther King, Jr, allowing him to claim some knowledge of justice in the situation he faced. What is more, the knowledge he claimed maintained the dialectical tensions of life, refusing – even in the wake of social barbarism – to bifurcate the world into the absolute evil of some over against the absolute goodness of others. Abraham Lincoln and Mahatma Gandhi accomplished similar feats of moral and cognitive courage. Likewise, an intellectual courage was evident not only in Einstein's willingness to 'challenge an axiom', but in his expressions of fear concerning the development of technical knowledge without a corresponding rise in social wisdom. And – if political cycnicism does not sweep away all such judgments – the intellectual leadership of Gorbachev may also represent a kind of cognitive courage, confronting as it does not only entrenched powers, but fossilized ideas.

The flight from ambiguity seems to be such an ancient human trait that it is enshrined in myth. Adam and Eve were tempted to escape the ambiguities of creaturely existence (being neither gods nor mere animals, yet aware of both) through a cognitive apotheosis (they would become like gods). The Tower of Babel (and perhaps the 'city' in these conflated parables) was built to overcome the ambiguity of human capacities (a mixture of life and death, power and limit). And the current flight from ambiguity leads also in the direction of technological soteriology. Why does humanity flee? We do not seem to live well with our status, caught, as one poet has it, between 'dust and divinity'. Humanity is tempted in both directions: to claim to be a child of pure spirit, or of pure nature. Both are wrong. As Reinhold Niebuhr argued in *The Nature and Destiny of Man*, if people insist that they are children of nature and 'ought not to pretend to be more than the animal', they must at least admit to being curious animals who make such assertions. Or if persons insist rather upon their 'unique and distinctive place in nature', they must suppress the anxious suspicion that they maintain an 'unconscious kinship with the brutes'.[2]

The confusion Niebuhr cites about how human beings are to understand themselves is evident in the debates over environmental ethics. Some within the technological mainstream still seem to regard nature as the enemy which must be conquered. Peter Medawar, for instance, expressed some perplexity that some persons had lost their technological nerve. Any problem caused by technology could be solved by technology.[3] Hannah Arendt once noted that the contemporary world was bent on replacing the world as given with the world as artefact. On the other side of the equation, some within the environmental movement locate the problem with the human tendency to regard itself as transcendent of nature. The 'deep ecologists', for instance, seem to value wild nature above human existence, if not merely on a par. Peter Singer speaks of 'speciesism' as a way of criticizing the preference for human life above the life of other creatures. Thus, one must choose for nature or against it, for spirit or against it. Both, from this perspective, are wrong. The cognitive and practical problem is to live creatively in the dynamic tension between human being as part of nature, and human being as transcendent of it in culture, morality and faith.

The failure to live creatively with the dialectical character of self and world has resulted in a kind of intellectual floundering in the contemporary era. More precisely, it has led to an intellectual 'cold war' rather than a new synthesis of subject and object. On each side of this war, combatants can be seen deriving their arsenals from the side of the subject to assault the object, or vice versa. The point is worth describing in a number of ways.

In recent theological discourse, for instance, ecological crisis has been seen to be 'caused' by male images of deity. Rosemary Ruether argues that the 'destruction of the earth and its environment' is 'inherent' in the fundamental patriarchal revolution of consciousness that sought to deny that the spiritual component of humanity was a dimension of the maternal matrix of being. Patriarchy sought to elevate consciousness to supernatural authority. Mother and nature religion traditionally have seen heaven and earth, gods and humans, as dialectical components within the primal matrix of being. Its spirituality was built on the cyclical ecology of nature, of death and rebirth. Patriarchal religion split apart the dialectical unities of mother religion into absolute dualism, elevating a male-identified consciousness to transcendent apriority.[4]

In spite of the language critical of the breaking of dialectical unity by 'dualism', in fact new dualisms are rife in this form of analysis. Male deity is identified as transcendent, while female deity is immanent. The former annihilates nature for transcendent history, while the latter maintains nature in the bonds of origin. The truly dialectical notion of God as transcendent Spirit immanently present in nature and history is itself annihilated. The polar understanding of reality has given way to anti-theses, one of which is morally, intellectually, and practically repugnant.

A concomitant problem is represented by recent attempts of literary theory and philosophy to place thought (quite properly) within the conditionality of history. In various forms of a 'hermeneutics of suspicion' (Paul Ricoeur), the texts of culture are analysed to discover within them the political, sociological and economic interests they serve. One seeks to discover the uses of power in a text (Foucault), or to find the way that sex, class and gender orientation give ideological sanction to ideas. One 'deconstructs' the text, but not ironically the one doing the deconstruction. The undialectical nature of such criticism has raised the same problem posed by earlier existentialism. In their revolt against the dominant, hierarchical, scientific-technological system, both existential and more contemporary protest movements fail to explain the 'miracle of epistemology' by which subjective, immediate and egalitarian ways of knowing gain universal validity. What prevents such critical thought from falling on the sword of its own criticism? If all knowledge is ideology, what intellectual (or moral) reasons are there for accepting the ideological (i.e. self-serving) claims of one group over another? One answer is that the social power of a given group will determine the 'truth' of its claims. But this is merely to collapse the notion of knowledge back into that of politics. The answer must point, rather, to the dialectics of nature and history, of ontology and dynamic life. The vicissitudes of power must certainly be analysed in every culture and in every era. The masks of ideology must be uncovered, whether of a dominant (or dependent) nation or sex or race. But the groundedness of human beings in a common reality must also be granted. The historical does not annihilate the ontological significance of humanity. For instance, Paul Tillich claims that '[t]he justice of a system of laws is inseparably tied to justice as conceived by the ruling group, and this justice expresses both principles of right and wrong and principles by which the ruling group affirms and sustains and defends its own power'.[5] The exercise of power is ambiguous, not merely demonic, not merely divine. The laws represent the interests of some segments of the community, but they also represent justice. They are ambiguous, not merely just or unjust. In this way, the dialectical task of thought remains to give each thing its due, to criticize injustice and self-serving action, but to search for the common ground of justice in a given society, in a given time.

The hegemonic tradition – which has been developing since the English Enlightenment – has contributed fundamentally to a related intellectual failure of modernity. By fostering the notion that all knowledge is of one stripe, disciplines that do not replicate the methods of mathematical natural science and the traditional 'ends' or '*teloi*' of human being they contemplate have been driven out of the cognitive realm. Only the 'means', the 'efficient cause', the instrumentalities are granted intellectual dignity. 'To a culture in which science represents the paradigmatic, if not the exclusive, mode of knowing,' argues Langdon Gilkey, 'knowledge is apt to be regarded as all on one level.'[6] If the only questions permitted intellectual dignity are ones that fit the model of science, then the ends of life have no standing. In Aristotle's terminology, one can no longer rationally appropriate that beyond which nothing greater can be imagined. The questions 'For what purpose?' 'To what significance?' are subjectified – left for individual tastes. Language concerning the good, the true, the beautiful; concepts of God, of love, and of justice have been largely relegated by the hegemonic intellectual tradition to the cognitive dustbin of emotion. As Bentham put it, 'It is by hopes and fears that the *ends* of action are determined; all that reason does is to find and determine the means.' Hence intellectual modernity (perhaps since Locke) has had to face a world without final meaning or grounding.

This is true not simply for those who have fostered the new myth of science of the universe as meaningless mechanism, but for those who have in revolt confirmed the same diagnosis. There is no objective ground for moral action, but humanity must struggle to ground the groundless (Camus). There is no human being in ontological terms, but one must be made in acts of freedom (Sartre). There may be no God, but human beings – for the sake of prudence – must act as if there were (James). The list is almost coincidental with contemporary thinkers. Perhaps this is why Allan Bloom charged in *The Closing of the American Mind* that the sole virtue taught in higher education for the past fifty years is 'openness', born of a passionate belief in 'relativism'. 'The point is not to correct the mistakes and really be right,' he argues, 'rather it is not to think you are right at all.'[7] The relevant antecedents for such claims are less mathematics or natural science than those forms of inquiry once thought to have a rational ground now victims of contemporary 'contextualization'. Without borrowing further from Bloom's analysis, the historical character of all knowledge should be realized, and at the same time a penetration to deeper levels of unity and coherence should be sought. If the traditional sin of cognition has been to turn anthropological experience into ontology, salvation does not reside in destroying the rational character of ends as such, or undermining the rational grounding of any *Wissenschaft* not directly expressing the model of mathematical natural science. When this happens, human purposes (and the interpretation of reality itself) are turned over to hidden, unconscious and perhaps irrational forces. Advertisers and political entities, for instance, may be quite happy not to have critical and rational competition in defining the ends of life.

A dialectical understanding must allow for the several ways of knowing the varied realities. Aristotle argued as much, warning that 'It is the mark of an educated [person] to look for precision in each class of things just so far as the nature of the subject admits; it is evidently equally foolish to accept probable reasoning from a mathematician and to demand from a rhetorician scientific proofs.'[8] Familiar epistemological problems such as 'reductionism' and the hegemony of 'linear' modes of knowing illustrate the problem of ignoring good – if ancient – advice. Methods should thus be 'autogeneous' (appropriate to their objects) rather than 'heterogeneous' (imperialistically encroaching upon their objects, grasping only a part rather than the whole).[9]

Intellectual failures occupy the self-understanding of human being as well as being itself. Can reality be understood as an aggregation of the parts, or as a whole? The very question defines more than a century of debate, and yet it is wrong in its very premise. As the environmental crisis illustrates, the deep nominalism of contemporary science – with its corresponding division of labour between scientists and between university departments – has blocked an adequate conception of the interdependent whole. Such a conception has been regarded by many within the academy as intellectually 'soft'. But, in reality, the earth is not merely a collection of discrete things, but a system, a process, and an interconnected whole.

Likewise, should human beings be understood in terms of individualism or collectivism? Are individuals thus free, or are they determined? Any antithetical answer does damage to the reality. Human beings are ambiguously free within a destiny, and are individuals formed by and forming human communities. To violate this vibrant tension is to break the ontological bond of humanity. Thus, if Robert Bellah and his colleagues can rightly question those *Habits of the Heart* that form the problems of 'individualism and commitment in American life',[10] then the ecstatic political outbreaks now taking place in Eastern Europe demonstrate the equal and opposite failure of collectivism to honour human being. And if the behaviourism of B. F. Skinner and his legions seems to violate notions of human dignity and freedom, then aspects of the human potential movement likewise appear to ignore the historical embeddedness of personhood.

Coping with humanity's failure to know, with its escape from ambiguity, will be a matter of grace embodied in forms of justice. But the courage to live between dust and divinity cannot merely be willed by persons or groups. Humanity does not summon its own ground. And yet, this is the 'theonomous' possibility in our time: that the unity and meaning of being may once again grasp humanity even while the analyses of the particularities of existence continue with ever-refined means.

Notes

1. Bernard Lonergan, *Three Lectures*, Montreal 1975, 549.
2. Reinhold Niebuhr, *The Nature and Destiny of Man*, New York 1964, Vol. 1, 1.
3. Peter A. Medawar, *The Hope of Progress*, Garden City 1973.
4. Rosemary Radford Ruether, *New Woman, New Earth*, New York 1983, 194f.
5. Paul Tillich, *Systematic Theology*, 3 vols., Chicago and London 1951–63, Vol. 3, 264.
6. Langdon Gilkey, 'Creationism', *Christianity and Crisis*, 26 April 1982, 111.
7. Allan Bloom, *The Closing of The American Mind*, New York 1987, 26.
8. *Nicomachean Ethics*, Book 1.5.
9. See Paul Tillich, *The System of the Sciences*, Lewisburg 1981.
10. Robert N. Bellah et al. *Habits of the Heart*, Berkeley 1985.

Religion as a Praxis for Coping with Contingency

Alois Müller

For around twenty years the definition of religion as a 'praxis for coping with contingency' has been current. As is well known, it comes from a functionalist theory of religion. Even those who do not agree with this characterization of the function of religion will at least have to concede that the approach to the problem of religion in terms of the concept of contingency represents a challenge to the philosophy of religion and opens up fruitful perspectives for research.

However, as I shall go on to demonstrate, an unambiguous clarification of the concept of religion is difficult, since this concept is disputed in all disciplines.[1] That is so not least because the concept of contingency is in fact itself ambiguous. It can be used theoretically in a variety of ways and often allows virtually opposite positions.

Whether religion and contingency have a conceptual affinity or whether the two terms are mutually exclusive depends not only on the interpretation of the concept of contingency but also on the definition of religion and its particular historical and social constitution.

What is 'contingency'?

Here I want to stress only three perspectives from the complicated and momentous history of the concept of contingency and its importance in the history of Western metaphysics.[2] First, the concept of contingency has its original context in logic, where it serves to provide a modal-theoretical distinction between the possible or fortuitous and the necessary. In the version generally accepted today, the contingent is defined in modal theoretical terms as that which is neither necessary nor impossible. If the concept of contingency is arrived at by the exclusion of necessity and impossibility, the contingent embraces everything that is possible otherwise. In the phenomenologically enlightened language of system theory, N. Luhmann puts it like this: the concept of contingency 'therefore denotes what is given (experienced, expected, thought, imagined) and which could possibly be otherwise; it denotes objects against the horizon of possible changes. It presupposes the given world, and thus does not denote the possible generally, but what could be otherwise, given reality. In this sense there has also recently been talk of "possible worlds" of the one real world of life. In the concept of contingency the reality of this world is thus presupposed as the first and irreplaceable condition of being possible.'[3]

Since Kant, in German contingency has often been defined as 'fortuitousness'. A corresponding definition of 'fortuitous' runs: 'The fortuitous is what, although it *is*, could also *not* be, and what although it is *so*, could also be *otherwise*.'[4]

Secondly, in the tradition of theological metaphysics the modal theoretical significance of contingency became allied with the non-necessity and the 'being of the entity which could also be otherwise', with the doctrine of creation and the question whether the existence of God can be proved. In interpretations in terms of the theology of creation, the concept of contingency took on the significance of 'dependent on', in addition to its modal-theoretical significance. Worldly things and all that is created were understood to be dependent on the omnipotence of God, which was seen as being supramodal. The idea of the *contingentia mundi* led to the cosmological proof of God. H. Blumenberg sums up the historical development in the following way:

> The Middle Ages found in the concept of contingency first the radical exegesis of the idea of creation, that concept which is one of the few genuine formations in the history of metaphysics of specifically Christian origin, although it had emerged from the Latinization of Aristotelian logic. Contingency determines the notion of a world created out of nothing and destined to pass away, held in existence only by the divine will, which is measured by the idea of an unconditioned and necessary entity.[5]

Thirdly, whereas Aristotle did not yet take into consideration contingency in the sense of the fortuitousness of all being, and even Hegel could say in his philosophy of history that the philosophical approach has 'no other purpose than to remove the fortuitous', our modern age which has come about lives in full awareness of a contingency that is neither metaphysical nor sublated in the theology of creation. The specifically modern 'experience of the *contingency* of human existence in the totality of the world' (K. Löwith) was already heralded in the seventeenth century, when the Christian metaphysical view of the world gradually began to collapse. The 'God of modern metaphysics' (W. Schulz) and the Christian liberal synthesis were then fatally affected by the nineteenth- and twentieth-century criticism of ideology and religion which proceeded by way of genealogy. The destruction of trust in the possibility of knowing 'eternal truths' introduced by Kant encouraged the discovery of historical contingency along with the construction of a scientific view of the self and the word. The experience of the *'contingence irréductible de l'histoire'*, as Lévi-Strauss put it, which is clearly articulated in present-day thought as culturalistic relativism, accentuated the crisis for all those religions which are built on tradition regarded as unquestionably valid and dogmas protected by the institution. The omnipresent awareness of contingency is perceived by many people as an opportunity for emancipation from outdated models of interpretation and models for action which cannot be believed in. However, the collapse of established cultural taxonomies and the *'révolutions du "croyable"'* (M. de Certeau) also produce anxiety and uncertainty. This 'fear of contingency' (Merleau-Ponty) can be read out of the totalitarian ideologies and religious, anti-modernistic orthodoxies which have arisen with modern times and which promise a stop to the unreasonable demands of the cognitive and emotional stress of a highly developed sense of contingency and offer security.

Three models

To gain a wider view of the actual and conceivable structures of religion and contingency I shall distinguish three models, each of which I shall illustrate by representative figures from the modern discussion. They are: 1. *The emancipatory model which is critical of religion*. Using the early Sartre, I want to show how the modern experience of contingency takes us away from Christian religion and metaphysics. 2. *The functional-analytical model which offers a foundation for religion*. This comes in two variants: Variant A puts the emphasis on the anthropological basis, arguing that religion is indispensable from the perspective of a pragmatic philosophy of culture. It is put forward by H. Lübbe. Variant B considers the problem of religion from the perspective of a more developed system theory. It denies that religion is anthropologically necessary, but claims that it is indispensable for society. I shall use N. Luhmann's theory as an example here. 3. *The utopian-aesthetic model*: in this model, as in the first, religion and metaphysics are rejected in the name of contingency. But here the awareness of contingency is not made tolerable by the ethic of authenticity, but is coupled with irony in the private sphere and solidarity in the public sphere. I want to present this model by means of the most recent book by the American philosopher R. Rorty.[6]

1. The emancipatory model which is critical of religion

The concept of contingency plays a decisive role in Sartre's first major work and also appears in his later work as a Leitmotiv. As early as in the introduction to his 'Attempt at a phenomenological ontology', which is the subtitle to *Being and Nothingness*,[7] Sartre defends the independence of being and rejects the theologoumena of *creatio ex nihilo* and *creatio continua*. The impossibility of deriving being-in-itself, its uncreatedness and superfluity, are precisely what makes up its contingency: 'Uncreated, without ground of being, without any relationship to another being, being in itself is superfluous to all eternity' (EN, 33f.). As J. Hengelbrock rightly stresses, the 'anti-religious intention of Sartre's ontology'[8] becomes clear from the way in which he takes over and reinterprets the metaphysical, creation-theological concept of contingency. It becomes quite evident from the following comparison which Hengelbrock makes: 'Just as the believer knows that he is sublated in God's hand, as he finds from God the meaning of his life and a task, so by contrast Sartre's human being finds himself "forsaken", nowhere sublated in his being, existing by chance and as superfluous as a stone in the road, not knowing what he should really do and what he is good for.'[9] In the journal-like notes in his novel *Nausea*, which according to the famous remark by Simone de Beauvoir is a meditation on contingency, Sartre makes his 'hero' Antoine Roquentin note in connection with his discovery of the relationless existence of the roots of the chestnut tree: 'Contingency is the essential thing. I want to say that existence is not necessity by definition. To exist is quite simply to be there; existents appear, can be encountered, but they cannot be derived. I think that there are people who have understood that. But they have attempted to overcome this contingency by inventing a necessary being which is its own foundation. No necessary being can explain existence; contingency is no deception, no appearance which one can drive away; it is the absolute, and consequently complete groundlessness.'[10] There is no room here for a proper discussion of Sartre's analysis of delusion and of human desires to be God which are condemned to failure (cf. EN, Part Two). Abbreviating the problem of the early Sartre for the philosophy of religion, which is also closely bound up with the idea of freedom, the thesis can be ventured that philosophical 'explanations' and the giving of religious meaning, the allegedly well-ordered world of representation and ceremonies, prevent that inexorable and illusion-free confrontation called for by Sartre with the enigmatic nature of the 'density of being', the superfluity of one's own existence which is transitory and for which there is no justification. The knowledge and recognition of '*gratuité*' and fortuitousness call for a farewell to a metaphysical-moral God, the '*Ens causa sui* which the religions call God' (EN, 770), the God-ideal which burdens the human conscience with permanent guilt. 'The intuition of our contingency' cannot be assimilated to a feeling of guilt; that is Sartre's objection to Heidegger, who seeks to reconcile his humanism with the religious sense of transcendence (EN, 118). That according to Sartre's philosophy inter-personal love is also a useless attempt to elevate contingency to an outline of meaning (cf. EN, Part Three) is a further example of Sartre's remoteness from the Christian interpretation of life. Rather than include Sartre in the literature of the absurd, a classification also favoured by theologians, here finally we should stress with E. Kaufmann that the early Sartre, too, already has a central concern with human liberation and the foundation of a new praxis.[11]

2. *The function-analytical model which provides a foundation for religion*
In this model, the anthropological, cultural and social function of religion is discussed. We turn first to Variant A, as it has been presented by H. Lübbe. In his main work on the theory of religion, *Religion nach der Aufklärung*,[12] the Zurich philosopher seeks to demonstrate why despite the success of the Enlightenment and the completion of secularization we may expect no end to religion. In so doing he takes the opposite position to the theory of the 'end of religion', as it is at present being developed, say, by M. Gauchet (*Le désenchantement du monde*, 1985) or G. Dux (*Die Logik der Weltbilder*, 1982).[13]

Lübbe is aware that the theory of the persistence of religion cannot be derived from the actual survival of religious orientations and organizations. The reason for the permanence of religious culture must be sought in a concept of religion which is so fundamentally present that it does justice to both the universality and the plurality of religious phenomena. Moreover, this theory has to stand up to the objections of a radical and genetic criticism of religion and therefore may not itself be reductionist. Lübbe now believes that in the definition of religion as a 'praxis for overcoming contingency' which he has been propagating for the past fifteen years, he has found a concept of religion which fulfils these conditions. In this formula, which is to be understood functionally, both meanings of the concept of contingency occur. The content of 'dependence on . . .' in the first place supports Lübbe's assertion of the anthropological and ontological need for religion. In the definition which I have mentioned, 'contingency' does not primarily denote any specifically modern experience, but the universal experience of human beings that they are dependent, non-autarkic beings, who do not owe their existence to themselves. In this context, contingency also means 'not being under our control'. Lübbe now asserts that human beings can lead their lives rightly only if they put themselves in a relationship to the contingent conditions of their existence outside their control that serves life. Human beings must accept without constant revolts the presuppositions of existence which they cannot either produce or change by intervening actively in reality. According to Lübbe, the basic function of religion lies in this unconditional assent to life, in the free and autonomous recognition of 'contingency which transcends the meaning of action'. The mark of irreligion and antireligion, which is expressed, for example, in totalitarian political ideologies, lies in the rejection of this contingency. Thus from a functional perspective religion – and everything that fulfils this function is religion! – fulfils 'a life-function of anthropological univerality' and denotes a 'praxis through which we establish a rational relationship to the contingency of our life and its conditions which are not at our disposal' (16). Lübbe is convinced that particularly at a time when our power to act is expanding, the 'culture of correct dealing with that which is not at our disposal' (279) needs especially to be nurtured and practised, because the pre-eminence of the paradigm of production gives rise to the illusion that we can progressively master all the conditions within which we act, and that gives rise to hubris. A humane society and a liberal state should therefore have an interest in sustaining all cultural institutions which can present contingency in a symbol and ritual form. The truth of these institutions, as of all religion, emerges in the way in which they serve life. Here Lübbe does not dispute that religions and cults can have destructive sides.

However, the modal-theoretical sense of contingency is also present in Lübbe's definition of contingency. The functional approach and the question of functional equivalences is itself an expression of historical contingency and the social conditioning of specific religious forms. Lübbe now thinks that, under the conditions of a post-Enlightenment culture in a secularized society, the experience of the historical contingency of religion can no longer be external: 'The historical external perspective has, in our modern times, long entered our religious and confessional cultures, and a reconstruction of a naive form of belief which includes a content formulated on the basis of the historicistic refraction of a free relationship to its content, expressed in the form of a confession, is inconceivable and can be seen only as a relic of an insular culture' (123). Therefore hermeneutics is unavoidable. Moreover, historical reason requires that what is seen to be historically fortuitous is not to be confused with what is purely arbitrary. Reflective distance from one's own tradition always also brings with it the task of a critical continuation of tradition.

But what would be worth keeping of Christianity if 'successful life' were 'made the criterion of the truth of religious orientation' (253)? What transformations would Christianity have to undergo if it were in fact to take over the 'role of a cultural patron of the Enlightenment' that is hinted at (73)? What Enlightenment is to be protected here, and by what means? I shall leave these questions open and go on to give a brief sketch of variant B.

The Bielefeld sociologist of religion N. Luhmann already associated the theme of the evolution of religious dogmatics with the problem of contingency in his first discussion of the theory of religion in 1972. Like the classics of non-Marxist sociology – Durkheim, Weber, Talcott Parsons – he too does not criticize religion in order to unmask it. But he does not deal with it apologetically, as does Lübbe. His question is, rather: how is religion possible in a highly complex, differentiated society which no longer allows any representation of itself as a whole, and what religious code may still be held to be significant in an individualistic culture of reflection? In developing his theory, Luhmann leaves aside the derivation of contingency from the theology of creation and concentrates wholly on the exhaustion of the modal-theoretical sense. With his conceptual apparatus from system theory he succeeds in giving a precise meaning to concepts which were vigorously disputed even in the theology of recent decades. So for example he understands 'secularization' as the 'social-structural relevance of the privatization of religious decision'.[14] The distinction between immanence and transcendence is understood as a central code of religion which leads to the moral codification of religion with the help of the pattern of salvation and damnation.[15]

In contrast to Variant A, Luhmann resolutely disputes that religion is anthropologically indispensable: the position held by many theologians. He writes: 'One can be born, live and die without participating in religion . . . The possibility of leading a life without religion cannot be disputed as an empirical fact, and the religious system is confronted with this fact. All the anthropological bases for the function of religion collapse over this fact; neither the need for meaning nor the need for comfort keeps religion alive.'[16] A scientific demonstration that religion is indispensable can only be given in connection with the communications system of society: 'Religion does not solve specific problems of the individual, but fulfils a social function.'[17]

It is worth keeping this difference from variant A in mind if Luhmann's short version of the function of religion, namely the transformation of indeterminate complexity into determinate complexity, is to become understandable. In a way which represents a challenge to theology, Luhmann now says that the concept of God must be understood as analogous to the formulations of contingency in other functional systems –

e.g. scarcity in economics – as a specific means of changing indeterminate contingency into determinable contingency. But the notion of contingency must be applied consistently to the concept of God and can no longer be blocked with the scheme of perfection. How will theologians react to the following remarks of Luhmann, who constantly reviews his theory with a wealth of examples from the history of religion and specifically also Christian theology:

> A Christian theology would have to renounce the additional myth of the resurrection and be able to say why this conversion of the questioning and negative direction on Golgotha (what he means is Christ's 'Why?' on the cross!) remains the last word – even for its God. Only if it can then still recognize its God in Jesus – without a happy end, without resurrection, without eternal life, without reward for his exemplary tenacity – only then would it have posed to itself the problem of religion.[18]

Here Luhmann touches on a point at which he agrees with Lübbe. Both are convinced of the failure of all attempts at a 'theodicy',[19] and both derive a strict distinction between religion and morality, between religion and politics, from this. However, according to Luhmann, the problems facing religion in modern society, in which traditional religious semantics has almost ceased to find any points of contact, are barely touched on with a neat distinction of a variety of ways of living and the establishment of guidelines. The question of the function and the code of religion is accentuated by an intensification of the awareness of contingency which leads to the 'unavoidability of a recursive observation of observations'.[20] The assumption that there are second-order conditions for observation excludes the idea of a privileged standpoint for the observation of the world in the world. In such a situation everything becomes controversial: the model of contingency is exposed to criticism, the latency of the encipherment of social contingency is disclosed, the points of contacts for what is unambiguously right are lost, and even the communication of faith becomes observable.

3. The utopian-aesthetic model

Many readers will presumably shrink from the relativistic consequences of functionalist system theory. Do not the last normative certainties vanish here?

I now want to refer to a thinker who is not afraid of relativism and who advises that contingency should be dealt with in a playful and ironic way. For R. Rorty[21] of the University of Virginia, the recognition of contingency means an insight into the conditioning of all linguistic games and the renunciation of an ultimate vocabulary, the recognition of the chance nature of the 'self' and a readiness constantly to weave anew the web of relationships of which we consist, and finally the concession that there are no ultimate foundations even for claiming that political and moral convictions are correct. According to Rorty, metaphysics, religion and theology are obsolete attempts to maintain continuities and efforts to disguise or stem contingency which are hopelessly doomed to failure. In Rorty's utopia of a completely de-divinized, liberal society the metaphysicians and priests would be replaced by the 'strong poets' who have no fear of contingency. The Christian ideal of self-fulfilment would give way to a permanent self-creation and re-description, and a 'poetized culture' would replace religious culture. The ironical intellectual would not make any claims to universality; the liberal-ironic citizen would be able to combine an experimental sense of dealing privately with contingency with a feeling of obligation in solidarity with others.

Conclusion

A philosophical and theological discussion of these models could only rightly begin after this survey. And there is room here only for a final consideration.

The introduction of the concept of contingency into the discussion of the theory of religion makes possible inter-disciplinary discussions and provides an opportunity of adding the problem of religion to the present state of awareness. Becoming sensitive to contingency marks an end to authoritarian and bureaucratic religious communication connected with the exercise of power. A perception of contingency which is free of anxiety excludes dogmatism and fundamentalism. It strengthens a sense of variety and poetry. It aims at an ethic which recognizes differences and otherness.

But the metaphysical model of contingency can also once again bring out the logic of dependence in the religious, political and social spheres. It could legitimate an ethic of subjection and surrender to fate. In a civilization abounding in dangers a 'bold fatalism without revolt' (Nietzsche) could offer itself as religion. In the sphere of the Bible and rabbinism an ontology of fate and a remythicized creation faith would then come into conflict with prophetism and the exodus tradition. The question of a reformulation of the basic religious codes compatible with the structure of society cannot be left merely to the religions and churches. It is a task for the whole of culture.

Translated by John Bowden

Notes

1. Cf. F. Wagner, *Was ist Religion? Studien zu ihrem Begriff und Thema in Geschichte und Gegenwart*, Gütersloh 1986.

2. Cf. 'Kontingenz', *Historisches Wörterbuch der Philosophie*, ed. J. Ritter, Vol. 4, cols. 1027–38, Basel and Stuttgart 1976. For further examples of the theme of contingency see my article 'Überlegungen zum Verhältnis von Religion und Kontingenz', in *Entwicklung von Religiosität*, ed. A. A. Bucher and H. Reich, Fribourg CH 1989, 35–50.

3. N.Luhmann, *Soziale Systeme*, Frankfurt am Main 1984, 152.

4. M. Sommer, *Identität im Uebergang: Kant*, Frankfurt am Main, 67.

5. H. Blumenberg, 'Selbsterhaltung und Beharrung', in *Subjektivität und Selbsterhaltung*, ed. H. Ebeling, Frankfurt am Main 1976, 165f.

6. R. Rorty, *Contingency, Irony and Solidarity*, Cambridge 1989.

7. J. P. Sartre, *L'Etre et le néant. Essai d'ontologie phénoménologique*, Paris 1943. There is an English translation, *Being and Nuthingness*, London 1969; page references are to the French (= EN).

8. J. Hengelbrock, *Jean-Paul Sartre*, Freiburg and Munich 1989, 62.

9. Ibid.

10. J. P. Sartre, *La nausée*, Paris 1938, 184f. There is an English translation: *Nausea*, London 1969.

11. E. Kaufmann, *Macht und Arbeit. J. P. Sartre und die europäische Neuzeit*, Würzburg 1988, 239ff.

12. H. Lübbe, *Religion nach der Aufklärung*, Graz, Vienna and Cologne 1986. The following quotations come from this book. There is a critical discussion of Lübbe's theory of religion and political philosophy in my article 'Religion, Kultur und Ethik unter Säkularisierungsbedingungen', in *Diskurs und Dezision*, ed. G. Kohler and H. Kleger, Vienna 1990, 85–313.

13. For the theological reaction to this theorem cf. P. Valadier, *L'église en procès. Catholicisme et société moderne*, Paris 1987.

14. N. Luhmann, *Funktion der Religion*, Frankfurt am Main 1977, 232.

15. N. Luhmann, *Gesellschaftsstruktur und Semantik*, Studien zur Wissenssoziologie der modernen Gesellschaft 3, Frankfurt am Main 1989, 250ff.

16. Ibid., 349.

17. Ibid.

18. Luhmann, *Funktion der Religion* (n. 14), 199.

19. Lübbe, *Religion nach der Aufklärung* (n. 12), 195ff.; id., 'Theodizee und Lebenssinn', *Archivio di filosofia* LVI, Rome 1988, 407–26 (on the theme *Teodicea oggi?*). According to Lübbe the problem of theodicy is 'religiously irrelevant', but not the problem of the meaning of suffering, which demonstrates the absence of any unquestioned significance for action and thus the need for religion in the sense of the acceptance of unconditional contingency. For contemporary attempts at a 'deconstruction' of theodicy see the volume mentioned above in this note.

20. N. Luhmann, *Die Unterscheidung Gottes: Soziologische Aufklärung 4*, Beiträge zur funktionalen Differenzierung der Gesellschaft, Opladen 1987, 251.

21. Cf. n. 6.

The Poetry of Failure – As Illustrated in German Post-war Literature

Karl-Joseph Kuschel

Prelude

Failure is regarded in particular circles as an expression of incompetence, as an often culpable neglect to meet claims, expectations or demands on the part of society. Those who fail have not achieved their aims, have suffered shipwreck. Their plans have come to nothing; their purposes have gone astray. In professional life people talk of 'failed existences', with the connotation that here someone is partly to blame for having gone under. In private life people talk of 'failed marriages' – with the clear connotation that here two people have disappointed the hopes originally set on them. In public life, there is talk of 'failed politicians' – as a rule not without malicious pleasure that their supposed incompetence has now fully come to light. If we want to sum up all these reactions, the answer is that in certain circles failure is identical with incompetence. The one who has failed is utterly incompetent, has the negative image of an existence which has fallen short, lost its function and become contemptible. The stereotype of failure may be fuelled by incompetence and contempt at the same time.

Counterpoint

One's first reaction to examining the literature of our time for a philosophical-psychological 'problem' chosen so much at random is one of resistance. To talk about 'literature' is like trying to put the sea in bottles or pack the wind in crates. Anyone who asks for such an examination would seem to have a fatal understanding of literature: as though literature were there to make abstract concepts concrete, to elaborate motives and provide themes with a little colour. Such attempts reduce literature to the function of illustrating the coloured stereotypes and texts of philosophical anthropology. Whereas confrontation with literature means giving up the idea that literature talks about a 'problem'. It happily leaves that to the philosophical essayists or journalists who write diagnoses of culture, since it knows that abstractions are the death of any literature.

The distinguishing feature of literature is that its world, especially the world of novels and plays, is populated by specific individuals, figures, persons. Each has a name, sex and age; each has a profession; each has an origin, comes and goes. Such individuals are called Claire Zachanassian or Mathilde von Zahnd (F. Dürrenmatt), Gantenbein or Stiller (M. Frisch), Oskar Matzerath or Eberhard Staruch (G. Grass), Fred Bogner or Leni Pfeiffer (H. Böll), Anselm Kristlein (M. Walser), Ricardo Fontana (R. Hochhuth) or Gesine Cresphal (U. Johnson). They come home dressed like millionaires or are doctors, blind people or sculptors, inmates of a mental hospital or student counsellors, telephonists, Jesuit fathers, housewives, trade representatives or translators. They live in Cologne or Danzig, Güllen or Rome, Berlin or New York, or they imagine themselves in fabulous places, which may be called Tynset or Masante, as in Wolfgang Hildesheimer. They are model figures of our history of consciousness, mirror-images of ourselves, archetypes of our collective capacity for memory. Their sphere is the counter-sphere, their world the para-world to our reality. By them we recognize who we are or could be.

So to avoid all abstractions, I shall not be talking here about failure as a 'motif', theme, or problem 'of literature', but of figures of failure *in* literature, of particular people as they inhabit the shadowy sphere of literature. And in order to structure the unending material and at the same time demonstrate a continuity of theme, I am choosing key texts from each decade of German post-war literature, so as first to give the theme a profile, after which I shall draw some general conclusions.

Scene 1: 1947

A man comes to Germany. He finds a girl, but the girl has a man who has only one leg and who constantly moans one name. The name is Beckmann. A door shuts and he stands outside.

A man comes to Germany. He is looking for people, but a colonel leaves him half-dead. A door shuts and he again stands outside.

A man comes to Germany. He is looking for work, but a director is cowardly. The door shuts and he again stands outside.

A man comes to Germany. He is looking for his parents, but an old woman is bothered about the gas. The door shuts and he again stands outside.

German literature after 1945, which has been called the literature of homecoming and ruins, begins as a literature of failure. The climax is

Wolfgang Borchert's 1947 piece 'Draussen vor der Tür', conceived as a radio play. Here the main figure is Beckmann, returning home from Russia after surviving the war and three years of imprisonment in Siberia; he now returns destroyed, a wreck in the ruined landscape of Germany. Scene by scene, here a man is introduced who belongs to a generation which is not only fanatical but also betrayed and cheated. While the soldiers became cannon fodder at the front, officers not only return as survivors but already come to terms with the new situation of the post-war period.

What really infuriates this limping homecomer with the black-rimmed eyes is not the many images of the dead which he cannot get out of his heart and mind, not the oceans of blood that he had to witness in the cauldron of Stalingrad, but the fact that the survivor no longer finds a place on this blood-soaked earth. Even the river into which he jumps spews him out again, and will not have this suicide. A colonel who during the war once foisted on to him the responsibility for a murderous reconnaissance patrol (eleven of his comrades had been killed) mocks him when the homecomer now wants to 'reassign the responsibility'. A director in whose cabaret he seeks a position with sad songs about the suffering of the war puts him off with excuses. A woman opens the door of his parents' home and tells him that the two old people have meanwhile committed suicide. And he finds his own wife, for whom he is looking, in the arms of another man. Truly Beckmann is 'one of those who come home and who yet do not come home, because they have no home'. And confronted with this situation Beckmann begins to take reckoning; to take reckoning with all the secret winners of the war, those who stayed at home and the happy repressors who do not think of interpreting the war as their own failure. But he also begins to take reckoning with the weak and impotently whining God who has handed his rule of the world over to death, who has had his fill of blood and corpses.

In other words, German literature after 1945 begins as literature of the failed in two senses of the word: the failed as victims of a war ideology and the failed as products of their vain repression. But Borchert's hero, despised though he is, still has the capacity to become an accuser and a rebel. Weary of life though he may be, he still has the strength to cry out his own failure as an accusation before God and the world. Here the one who has failed is not a failure but a victim, who calls in vain for an answer. But as a victim he becomes a rebel against those who bought their good post-war conscience by looking away.

Scene 2: 1957

A man is waiting in an Athens hospital for a life-and-death operation. And while he is waiting, he gives an account of the last three and a half months of his life. They were chaotic enough, not to be compared with any of the time that he had spent previously in the employment of UNESCO as a Swiss technician travelling round the world. Blow by blow, 'chance happenings', 'strokes of destiny', had intervened in the life of this man which hitherto had been under such control, in the life of a technologist who steadfastly refuses to believe in providence and fate because as a technician he is accustomed to consider life in terms of the statistics of probability. First comes the plane crash in the New Mexico desert which he survived; however, in it 'by chance' he got to know the brother of a former friend. Then comes the discovery that this former friend had committed suicide in the Guatemalan jungle; then the meeting with a young girl on a voyage to Europe. She becomes the man's lover but later proves to be his physical daughter, of whose existence he had no inkling. Then this girl dies on a journey to Greece and he has a reunion with his former betrothed in Athens; then he collapses on a filming trip with migraine. He is taken to an Athens hospital, and there his account, his 'unburdening', begins.

This is the story of a man with the codename *Homo faber* (Max Frisch, 1957) who – although subjectively innocent (what could *he* do about all the chances?) – cannot get over his guilt feelings about his incest and the death of his own daughter, and who now writes because he obsessively maintains his own innocence.

Why does Max Frisch tell this story in 1957? One thing is certain: unlike Borchert, Frisch does not use the failure of his hero to protest in an accusation against God and the world, but to raise self-critical questions about a life lived in the wrong way. With the figure of *Homo Faber* the mechanisms of unburdening and exculpation used by our modern contemporaries are disclosed; their boasts of innocence, their quest for unburdening, their failure generally are conceded. The novel holds up a mirror to a particular type of the time: it is demonstrated by a model case (skilfully constructed) that the assumption of ignorance does not bring about any unburdening of guilt and that self-justification can be based on the repression of guilt. If Borchert's innocent hero still rebelled against those fortunate ones who repressed their failure, Max Frisch's hero ten years later belongs to those who repress their own failed ideology: that of the technological control of the world. Precisely that might have been the strategic aim of Max Frisch's narrator; far from even hinting at a solution in the novel itself, the author is interested only in the dilemma of his hero: in the discrepancy between subjective-rational insight (innocence) and objective-irrational givenness (guilt on the basis of incest and death); in short, in the open scissors of guilt.

The novel is about these scissors of guilt. They are what give it its tension. The aim is to demonstrate that a person of the 'Homo Faber' type, millions of whom are present among us, is incapable of breaking out of the prison of his ideology and accepting self-critically a reality which escapes his plausibility. What is the guilt of Walter Faber? It may lie in his inability to accept the disruptions in his life caused by anything unplanned, fortuitous and unforeseeable as the occasion for a change of life, a change of life which not only, as in the last part of the novel, when Faber gets out, is a result of exhaustion or sickness, but of a new basic attitude to reality generally. So here is a demonstration of the inability of a person of power and potential to accept a reality which escapes his control: 'This man lives past himself,' says the author himself of his fictional character, 'because he is running after an image on general offer, that of "technology". Basically the *Homo Faber*, this man, is not a technologist but a handicapped man who has made an image of himself, who has allowed himself to make an image which prevents him from coming to himself.' So this inability to come to himself despite the experiences of disruption to his own life is what comprises the guilt of the 'innocent' Walter Faber. Here the one who has failed becomes the prototype of the innocent guilty one, who burdens himself with unburdenings of guilt, represses his false life and is unable to recognize failure as a chance to change his life.

Scene 3: 1963

When Heinrich Böll's novel *Faces of a Clown* appeared in 1963, there was no longer any trace of the Borchert-type ruined Germany. On the contrary, the land of homecomers and ruins had in the meantime become a Christian-Democrat state under Adenauer which had experienced an 'economic miracle', a country in which the Catholic Church was part of a firm power-cartel with a particular Christian party. Into this scenario of a land ignoring its past, disguising its guilt, self-righteously celebrating its economic successes, Heinrich Böll does not introduce anyone who is successful and *arriviste*, but an outsider and fool, who is himself the son of an *arriviste* industrialist: Hans Schnier, who is an actor, a clown.

But Hans Schnier is an outsider and fool not only in his work but above all in his remarkable understanding of love and marriage. The disturbing element of this novel and its criticism of government lies less in its political criticism than in the love story which forms the real framework for the action. From the time he was twenty-one, Schnier had lived with his girl-friend Marie. Although he was not religious, he regarded Marie – to some degree as any good Catholic would – as his wife. Indeed he had gone through marriage with her; for him her love in fact had the character of a self-given 'sacrament' which no one may attack, least of all church functionaries who actually attach importance to the element of self-giving in the sacrament of marriage.

However – not least under the pressure of church functionaries and the Catholic milieu – Marie had left Hans Schnier because, when the possibility of a Catholic wedding arose, he refused to promise that the children would be brought up Catholics, and she had married a 'progressive Catholic'. Schnier now attempts to get Marie back no matter what. After she left him, things also went downhill with him professionally; he began to drink, injured himself in his act as a clown and had to take a rest. But his fight and the return of his 'wife' are like the foolish fight of the 'knight with the sorrowful countenance' against the windmills. In the end the clown ends up a failure, a fool among fools, in the midst of the Rhineland carnival procession. Made up as a clown, no longer distinguishable from all the other clowns around him, he sits on the steps of Bonn railway station and gently and melancholically sings to the guitar the fool's song of 'Poor Pope John'.

So here we have a Böll scene from 1963: into the untroubled landscape of prosperous citizens, party bigwigs and church officials who are doing their best for themselves in the post-war period, Hans Böll puts a failure, a fool who cannot forget, a man who says of himself: 'I am a clown and collect moments'.

But this dialectic is important for the author: folly, madness and failure are a sign, not of the clown, but of society itself. The failed person is a fool not least because he lives in a crazy society, a society which reacts to the pressure of conformity by deviation and regards visions of love and self-given sacramentality as folly. But in this novel the mask of the clown serves to unmask others: the one who 'fails' discloses the failure and guilt of church and society, which misuse the clown's failure to confirm themselves. That might be the political strategy of this novel: the failure of the individual (presented as a love story) is basically the failure of a society which cannot tolerate this type of individual and must fend him off as a fool. On the appearance of this novel a critic wrote: 'The clown Hans Schier fails, but the moment of his failure achieves more than a victory, for it affects us like personal guilt' (G. Blöcker).

Scene 4: 1971

A good ten years after the appearance of the clown novel the political and literary scene in Germany had once again changed completely. In the meantime a politically radicalized student movement had discovered all that had been repressed in the Adenauer period and been disguised by a conservative mentality. The consequence, for literature also, was that centre-stage there was no longer occupied by a foolish outsider as with Böll, but by bourgeois society itself, the repressive behaviour of which was not only to be revealed but to be exploded by revolution. The Marxist writer Peter Weiss had already taken an active part in this revolutionary process of transformation with pieces like *The Song of the Ghost of the Lusitania* (1967), *Discourse on Vietnam* (1968), and *Trotsky in Exile* (1970).

In 1971, however, the student movement had already passed its peak. The first disappointment set in; bourgeois society proved tougher than had been expected, the revolutionary impulse began to ebb and the transformation of society into a Marxist utopia did not take place. Peter Weiss reacted to this situation with a 'historical drama', *Hölderlin* (1971). Even more radically than Borchert, Frisch or Böll, in this piece Peter Weiss accentuates the problem of failure in literature. Here we no longer have the failure as a rebel, as the innocent guilty one repressing his failure, as a fool: here we have a failure as voluntary self-sacrifice in the revolutionary battle. In the background of the Hölderlin piece stands the fate of the Cuban revolutionary Che Guevara, who had left Cuba voluntarily for the jungles of Bolivia to create a revolutionary consciousness among the peasants and agricultural workers there. Che Guevara's death in autumn 1967 had made Peter Weiss ask the basic question: what can be the significance of a voluntary sacrifice in the face of the existing control of power? May the individual also want to calculate the strategic significance of his failure for the cause?

Peter Weiss gives this problem parabolic form in his Hölderlin story. For in Hölderlin (for Weiss a crypto-Jacobin revolutionary) he had similarly come across the figure of a revolutionary who sacrificed himself, in Hölderlin's 'imaginary Empedocles fragment'. Fascinated by its sudden topicality, Peter Weiss confesses: 'Empedocles, swallowed up in Hölderlin's world, for me today, moreover, swallowed up in the world of Che Guevara, continues to make his central statement.'

And so in his Hölderlin play the dramatist stages a 'play within a play'. At the beginning of the second act Hölderlin has summoned his friends Hegel, Neuffer, Schelling, Schmid and Sinclair to Homburg (1799) to explain to them one last time, now almost in desperation, with the help of his Empedocles parable, the political action which is necessary, given the situation in Germany. Hölderlin beseeches his friends that just as Empedocles, this great philosopher, natural scientist, architect and physician of the state of Agrigento voluntarily left the people who wanted to make him king at the foot of the volcano Etna in Sicily, because this would not have changed the social structures, so too the intellectual élite in Germany must undermine the existing power structures. Indeed, just as Empedocles resolved to leave the city and go up the mountain as a signal to arouse the people from its political lethargy, so too the intellectual élite in

Germany must wage political warfare to arouse the people. And as Empedocles was not afraid of self-sacrifice when – betrayed by some of the people and pursued by state troops – he threw himself into Etna, so too if need be the intellectual élite in Germany had to act in the same way. However, Hölderlin's friends refuse to follow 'this idealist', and Hölderlin puts his view to the test. Like Empedocles, he too voluntarily throws himself into the abyss, but here the abyss of madness, and from now on spends his own life as a failure in the tower in Tübingen.

So what can be the significance of revolutionary self-sacrifice; what can be the strategic significance of failure? Peter Weiss's answer is that the individual can contribute to rekindling the revolutionary fire which has been quenched or 'only glimmers on in the individual' by 'extraordinary action'. So the individual need not be limited to the 'idea' of revolution: to some degree he or she can escape 'from the idea' and demonstrate what it would amount to in practice. Here this demonstration is fundamental. It offers the possibility of making a link backwards with a group for which this action takes place in exemplary fashion. The failure may not isolate himself, but must become 'a model for the one who comes after him'. And it is the task of these successors to justify the failure by revolutionary work for a better future. The individual may fail, but his cause remains undefeated.

Scene 5: 1986

Ingeborg Drewitz's novel *Eingeschlossen* (Shut In) sounds like an answer to Peter Weiss's strategic play about the self-sacrifice of the revolutionary. In the steps of Thomas Mann's *Magic Mountain*, Alexander Solzhenitsyn's *Cancer Ward*, Stefan Heym's *Collin* and Heinar Kipphardt's *März* (1976), Ingeborg Drewitz also utilizes the scenario of a hospital to depict the counter-world of the broken and failed. Two men meet in this clinic; both had set out to alter the world, indeed to improve it. One, the older man, a physician, had gone to America via Vienna and Zurich in the 1930s and later – for anti-Fascist motives – had collaborated in the development of the atomic bomb at Los Alamos. He had sought radical individual freedom for himself and only later noted what he had brought about through the atom bomb. The other, younger, man, born to a refugee towards the end of the war, had been a spokesman in the student movement and later a social worker. By his conduct and his speeches he had sought to convince, indeed to carry along, others and had attempted to follow the way of goodness, patience and endurance. But the 'march through the institutions' failed. Both are failures, both are broken. And both meet in the middle of the 1980s in the closed division of a Berlin psychiatric clinic, in which they tell each other their stories.

Only at a very late stage does Ingeborg Drewitz give us the full names of the two heroes. J and P are the letters used for them, and we are very soon aware that both figures are to serve as symbols. They stand for two basic patterns and models of human thought and action; they incorporate basic principles, force and counter-force: the Prometheus principle on the one hand (power, the will to impose and dominate) and the Jesus principle on the other (goodness, patience, which becomes a victim).

And yet this novel is not about a simple dualism of force and counter-force. The author knows that defects also appear in each of the characters: the crippling of the Prometheus element in the one, of the Jesus element in the other. And however much the author ultimately takes sides with the Jesus principle, she is nevertheless concerned to give a differentiated portrait of both characters: 'I was concerned in the strange movement between the two figures to point beyond guilt and existential anxiety to a tiny degree of sorrow and a cautious reconciliation of the principles that I have described. Beyond the abyss. The absurdity of the shutting-up of P and J also helped me to depict and put in question the brutal self-confidence of the "always doing it this way" in our everyday institutional life.'

Here Ingeborg Drewitz is not talking of failure either in the sense of revolutionary pathos or in terms of political recipes. The rebellious element of a Borchert, the paradox of a Frisch, the folly of a Böll or the revolutionary of a Weiss is alien to her. Her reflection on failure has the character of melancholy mourning on what is unreconciled and neglected. Reflection on failure leads to a structural problem: both heroes have to fail because they have either betrayed the Jesus principle in themselves or crippled the Prometheus principle. Both point beyond themselves to a utopia of reconciled opposites, the fulfilment of which is still to come.

Here, then, are five scenes, each with a different profile of failure. The striking thing is that what originally may have been a philosophical-psychological problem artificially introduced into literature proves on closer inspection to be a central and basic problem which appears as a motif. Through significant key texts of all the decades of German literature after 1945, there runs the thread of the failed hero. Indeed failure becomes *the* productive counter-experience of the writer in a society which seems secure. From here it would be an easy task to reconstruct the history of Germany after 1945 as a history of constantly new and continually different failure. After Franz Kafka, Robert Musil, Herman Hesse, Thomas Mann and Herman Brock, for the literature after 1945 the basic aesthetic axiom again is: it is above all the brokenness of our understanding of reality which seems capable of being expressed in literature, the hermeneutic of conflict which becomes aesthetically productive. The failed heroes of literature become the seismographs of a society which still awaits its reconciliation. So the first basic thesis which emerges is that the failed heroes of German literature after 1945 are figures who resist, who make things clear and who point beyond themselves. Precisely in its strongest representative, German literature after 1945 is a poetry of failure.

And yet we must locate our problem at an even deeper level. For the writers of our time do not only show failing heroes *in* literature. The greatest of the writers have always kept an awareness that failure is *immanent* in literature, indeed seems to be of the very essence of literature. Great authors were always conscious of the paradox that literature nowadays can succeed only by failing. And precisely the greatest of writers were not spared the experience that literature never escapes the dialectic of failure and victory with language and through language. Reality is greater, more complex, than what the author can express through language. Literature constantly falls short, does not leap far enough, attains only the fragmentary. All the novels of Franz Kafka remain fragments, not only because the author died 'too early' at the age of forty-one, but because self-doubt in the meaning of his writing had long left its mark on him. Robert Musil's great novel *The Man without Properties*, on which he worked for decades, also remained a torso. Thomas Mann's novel *Felix Krull* remained unfinished – despite all his efforts over forty years. And Heinrich Böll once acknowledged in connection with a novel of Christ to be written in the twentieth century: 'I do not believe that I am capable of writing such a novel. There are continual approximations but more than that is impossible.' In other words, there is not only a story of failed heroes in literature; a story could also be told of the history of *failed projects*, of the history of non-literature; a story could be told of non-stories, of linguistic scepticism, inability to speak, linguistic impotence, linguistic impediments and linguistic sorrow.

It is particularly the lyric poets among authors who have constantly revealed again the paradox of literature: that the scenario of the failure of language can be a form of successful literature. As an example I choose a poem by Günter Kunert, 'Vain attempt' (from *Still Life*, 1983):

In addition to all earthly torments
this: Not to find the word
the brain choked with dumbness
the look turned away and out:
rows of window panes
like insoluble crossword puzzles

Involuntarily the fingers touch
the stuff
of which the world is made
cheap material
nothing for eternity:
Neither flesh nor blood
neither arteries nor veins
not even the dazzling paper
full of expectation full of threat
of forgetting you
if you do not give it the word
that you do not have.

This poem is a symbolic portrait of the basic situation of the lyric poet in the twentieth century. For the situation of the artist with words is actually made more acute by the fact that he or she has to survive the crisis of language in addition to all 'earthly torments', that he or she experiences the situation of dumbness as conscious inability to speak – in the face of a reality which is like 'insoluble crossword puzzles'. Indeed there is more: the situation of the writer is made more acute by the fact that in the face of a world in which 'nothing is for eternity', even literature cannot be given the value of eternity. On the contrary, the empty paper before which the writer constantly sits is 'full of expectation' and 'full of threat' that it will leave him to be forgotten. And yet even the poem by Günter Kunert does not escape the paradox that the dumbness experienced before 'the word' once again needs speech to make it 'audible' at all.

This experience of the need for language and scepticism about language, about the power of literature and despair over it, represents the deeper dimension of failure in the literary sphere. In his first diary (1946–1949), Max Frisch expressed this situation in unsurpassedly lucid sentences:

What is important: what cannot be said, the white between the words, and the words always talk of incidental things that we do not really mean. Our concern, what is authentic, can at best be paraphrased, and that means quite literally that one writes around it, one transposes it. There are statements that never contain our real experience, which remains ineffable; they can only delimit it, as accurately and exactly as possible, and the real substance, that which cannot be said, at best appears as tension between these statements. Our effort is presumably to express all that can be said; language is like a chisel which cuts out all that is not mystery, and all statements involve a removal . . . There is always the danger that one shatters the mystery, and similarly the other danger that one stops too soon, that one leaves it a lump, that one does not pose the mystery, does not grasp it, does not free it from all that could be said, in short, that one does not penetrate to the ultimate surface.

These sentences in fact identify key experiences of writers of contemporary literature and describe the structure of failure as a principle. None of the great lyric poets experienced this more bitterly than Paul Celan. More than anyone else, he was aware of the fact that a poem today – as he said – 'displays a marked tendency to go silent'. He was convinced that the poem asserts itself today 'at the margin of itself'; it calls itself and brings itself in order to be able to exist, 'unexposed from its already no-longer back into its still-always'. So Paul Celan was in search of what he called the 'language of silence', a language which through and with language respected the wordless as the deepest ground of reality. Paul Celan called such poems for which he strove and at which he failed 'absolute poems', but he was quite clear about the paradox of this undertaking: 'The absolute poem – no, there is certainly no such thing; that cannot be. But with any real poem there is, with the most unpretentious poem, this unavoidable question, this unheard-of claim.'

So the second basic thesis which emerges is that German literature after 1945 does not just portray heroes who fail. It also preserves the awareness that – given the unbridgable discrepancy between language and reality – the failure of all literature is immanent. The awareness of the discrepancy between language and reality does, however, lead to the paradox that literature can only succeed as a failure, and any success points beyond itself to the absolute, that which is above language, that which cannot be put into words. The strongest representatives of German literature after 1945 not only present a poetry of failure; they also contain a poetic of failure.

Translated by John Bowden

II · Experiences

The Ethic of Failure and Beginning Again

A forgotten perspective in theological ethics

Dietmar Mieth

At a conference at the Paulus Academy in Zurich in 1987 I had the opportunity to talk at length with more than 100 people, the majority of them women, who had experienced failed marriages. I shall begin from these experiences of people who have been involved. I shall attempt to introduce the perspective of a theologian into what they said or what I heard in such a way as to make possible an encounter between the convictions of these Christian women and men as they have been lived out in practice and the living tradition of our knowledge of faith.

What is the perspective of the theologian? According to I Cor. 13.2, 'If I have faith without love, I am nothing.' For me, when applied to the theme of failure and beginning again, that means that God is love, in other words, that before God all individuals are worth more than they are to themselves and more than they are to others. That is the basic statement of Christian belief in God: God is love, and what God's love is is expressed in a revelation in which God has a history with human beings, in which he continually gives them more value.

I shall introduce this perspective into the experiences and practical convictions. This will give my comments the following structure: 1. The analysis of experiences of failure, in which I attempt to find a 'common denominator'; 2. A survey of attempts to work out these experiences; and 3. The ethic of beginning again: discovering a new life.

I. The common denominator of experiences of failure

1. Failure is the irrevocable destruction of a life
Here it should be noted that our lives develop on different levels. Human

beings have three non-physical basic needs: the need for successful personal relationships, the need for social recognition, and the need for meaning in life. Thus what seems to have failed on one level, and which draws in the other needs, is the fulfilment of the need for successful personal relationships. It is impossible for such a need to fail without other needs being involved in sympathy, like the need for social recognition and the need for a meaning in life behind which there is also the need for a relationship to God.

Failure is irreversible. The characteristics of failure are irreversibility and irrevocability. Crises can be surmounted, problems can be solved. But when we speak of failure we mean something that is irrevocable, even if we know that not everything fails with the failure of personal relationships or a failure of social recognition or a failure to find an answer to the question of meaning.

We learn from this that all failure is irrevocable, but not everything fails at the same time. Failure need not be total. If we introduce the Christian perspective of the love of God into failure as the irrevocable tearing apart of a marriage or a relationship, then we immediately find a statement which is very important: the person who fails is not rejected. Let us remember the basic perspective: human beings are worth more before God than they are to themselves. We know of a man who squandered his calling in a story of adultery and murder involving Bathsheba and Uriah. His guilt was held up to him by the prophet, but he was not rejected by God. And there is another example: in Matthew only five verses separate the calling of Peter as the rock of the church (16.18) from the cursing of Peter as Satan (16.23). Peter constantly fails: he fails here because after Jesus' prediction of his passion he offers the wrong advice, what Jesus calls the advice of the devil; he fails in the story of his denial; he fails over the question of bringing Jewish Christians and Gentile Christians together, and Paul has to make this clear to him by resisting. There is as much experience of failure as anyone could want in the question of what a relationship to God means. But from a Christian perspective it has to be stressed once again that the failed person is not rejected, and indeed can even have a special call and election.

2. An idea of success goes with failing

We cannot regard anything as a failure unless we have some idea of what success would be. This idea can be more or less conscious, more or less thought-out. This truth is as important as it is simple; for only through our ideal of a successful life, even in our personal relationships, can we have the contrasting experience that something has failed.

Here I would immediately want to add that failure is sometimes associated with a false idea of success, with false ideals. The falser the ideal, the more likely the failure. The ideal becomes false if it goes beyond reality, and the greater it appears, the greater is the suffering caused by reality. We must ask ourselves whether we can really experience the failure of questionable ideals as failure. As examples one could cite a series of questionable ideals of marriage which have been put forward in the church or which predominate in society. They begin from conceptions which, since they are one-sidedly idealized, cannot in fact succeed and therefore to some degree programme failure in advance.

As I have said, failure includes some idea of success. Therefore one important question is whether we have the right idea of success. Whether we do or not determines whether we also have the right attitude to possible failure. In my view the answer can only be arrived at by confronting superficial ideas in society and by looking critically at ideals in the church.

3. The experience of failure includes the ultimate impossibility of answering the question 'Why?'

In the end I cannot answer the question why I love someone, why I love my wife, in such a way that the answer can be objectified and transferred to any man; otherwise in the end all men would love my wife. I can give only a partial, plausible explanation. The question why I love cannot be answered, and similarly I believe that the question why people fail cannot be answered either. Why has a relationship failed? I at any rate could not give a final answer for others or for myself. There may perhaps be partial answers which take us so far, but whether it is put in the positive or the negative, the question 'Why?' ultimately remains unanswerable; and one of the reasons why suffering in failure is so painful is that we cannot answer the question why, even if we are quite ready to mourn.

I do not want to see this just in connection with the psychological dimension. The phenomenon also belongs in the religious dimension. This can be explained from a comment by Dorothee Sölle, which relates to her own experience. She is speaking of her experience of dying in connection with her divorce:

This death (the death of a relationship) was for me the complete destruction of a first life. Everything on which I had built, all that I had hoped for, believed, wanted, was destroyed. The experience is probably similar to that of the death of someone one loves very much. Except that in the story of a marriage and a separation the element of guilt necessarily plays a greater part and the awareness of having forgotten something, neglected it and got it irrevocably wrong cannot be assuaged by any form of belief in fate. It took me three years, not to come to terms with it, but to overcome the suicidal fantasies which constantly dogged me. Wanting to die was my only hope, my only thought. In this situation I once went into one of those old Gothic churches on a journey through Belgium. The expression 'pray' now seems to me to be wrong. I was one lonely cry. I cried for help, and behind it I could imagine two things: that my husband would come back to me, or that I would die and this constant torture would finally cease. In this church, submerged in my cry, a saying from the Bible occurred to me, 'Let my grace be enough for you' (*Die Hinreise*, Stuttgart 1975, 42f.).

Sölle illustrates this very experience of being able to answer the question 'Why?', but also the experience of mercy and being accepted, not being rejected, even though the question is not answered. She goes on:

I began to an infinitesimal degree to accept that my husband was going another way, his own way. I had come to the end and God had torn up the first plan. He did not comfort me like a psychologist, who would have explained to me that this was foreseeable. He did not offer me the usual social consolations; he threw me face down on the floor. It was not death that I wanted for myself, nor was it life either. It was another death. Later I noticed that all those who believe limp a little, like Jacob after he had struggled with the angel. They have already died once. One cannot wish this on anyone, but one cannot attempt to spare them the lesson either. There is as little substitute for the experience of faith as there is for the experience of love' (ibid., 43f.).

It seems to me that these words express real wisdom, which does not take a superficial view but arises out of deep suffering.

4. Various guilt-feelings go with the experience of failure

These feelings begin with a question to oneself: what have I done wrong? There is a bad conscience which is not just caused by an obvious action, as for example in the case of the husband who goes off; the one left behind also has a bad conscience: did I do something to drive him or her out? The guilt feeling is as it were a reflector for the experience of failure and does not in itself indicate in any moral sense the degree to which I am guilty or not. Guilt feelings can be false; they need to be clarified in a conscientious concern for myself. These feelings are also diffuse because they follow from a mixture of wrong developments and wrong decisions (some things have gone wrong and some things have been done wrongly) – and all this is bound up with the impossibility of giving an answer to the question 'Why?'. All that can be said is that I was one factor, the circumstances were another and you were a third. At some point I have to accept the web of things that went wrong and wrong decisions. Once a carpet has been woven, I cannot unweave it into individual threads, even if I can follow the trace of some dark colours.

Objectively, too, the way in which what went wrong is interwoven with wrong decisions makes feelings of guilt so vague. The failure of the right kind of life for which I have striven always involves a mixture of objective and subjective guilt. In moral theology we speak of objective guilt where an action or a state does not correspond to perceived and recognized norms. For example, not to tell the truth while accepting the norm that human beings must be honest with one another would be an objective fault. On the other hand there is a subjective accountability which makes guilt guilt. Contravention of a norm does not in itself amount to guilt. Subjective guilt only arises when I have to recognize myself as inescapably guilty before my conscience. That is not always the case. How can I solve the problems of accountability in a relationship after the event? These difficulties are one of the reasons why the sacrament of penance in private confessions is now in crisis in the Catholic Church. The complications often cannot be disentangled in the way presupposed by traditional moral doctrine in the church.

5. No two experiences of failure are the same

This statement became clear to me in the stories which were told in the groups at the conference mentioned above. Why are experiences not the same? Because conditioning by life-histories, families and social circumstances are different. I believe that someone in a better social situation, say a woman with financial security or a job, experiences this failure in a different way from someone in a worse social situation – to give just one example. Moreover the intensity of the experience of failure varies enormously depending on the previous life and social background of the person concerned. Indeed, the negative scale in experience is infinite. It can sink to such a depth that there is not only the 'death of a relationship', but this death of a relationship becomes psychological murder. In her novel *Malina*, which is about this problem, among others, Ingeborg Bachmann has depicted the break-up of a woman which comes about as a result of the dissolution of her self into a complete, as it were male, objectification. The experience of failure is certainly never the same, but it is more widespread than men or women usually believe. I think that it is important for us to bear in mind that the premature death of a partner also destroys a life. The rending of a life is experienced with the same intensity when a husband dies early, if for example a wife is robbed of her husband by cancer in her forties. If she had dreamed of a shared future, had wanted them to grow old together, this is already an irrevocable shock. And for a mother bringing up her children by herself the situation is the same whether she is divorced or living as a widow.

6. No one fails alone

No one fails alone in a relationship. Anyone who is aware of responsibility thinks, 'Who is failing with me?' The thought might be of the children, but it also might be that the person from whom one is separated is also failing, even though that is perhaps not so obvious, because the other person is perhaps entering into a new relationship.

The question is, if it is the case that no one fails alone in a relationship, can a husband and wife come to an understanding with each other? At the same time they also need to work out a common element in the separation which brings out the fact that they are both sharing in the experience of failure. For it is important for parents to arrive at something they have in common beyond the separation, so that there can be a new basis for that part of their relationship which still survives.

Finally, it is important in this context to understand the other person's failure as one's own suffering or to limit any personal indignation one feels by this understanding of the other person. Of course there is the French proverb, 'To understand everything is to forgive everything.' But that is a danger: if I show too much understanding I may be suppressing myself, my self-respect. A limit to understanding is set by self-esteem, which is extraordinarily important. There is a good deal to balance out: in this case a justified sense of self-esteem on the one hand and the need for understanding on the other.

7. Failure is never completely healed, but one can live with it

This experience differs with individuals, but I think that it is very important for failure not to be covered over with false hopes and false expectations and for no repression to be allowed. Failure also requires husband or wife to keep the wounds open so that they are not infected by repression. Husband or wife should not suppress the capacity to feel, and should sink into the depths of suffering without masochism or self-torture. However, who can really draw the boundaries clearly? It is, however, important to be perceptive, to sink into oneself without masochism and self-torment. What is not fully healed must also be present in one's life. Let us recall with Dorothee Sölle the three years she needed to get out of her suicidal fantasies and the limping Jacob represented by those who fail and struggle to understand their failure. A condition of being able to live with the wounds of failure is to make the right compromises in the face of the this situation, and that is a matter of working out failure.

II. How do we work out experiences?

I think that it is important, step by step, to make possible and to pursue the following insights and experiences.

1. I am a limited being

Working out the experience of failure means discovering that one is a creature. The theological term for 'to be a finite and limited being' is 'to be a creature', i.e. not to be God, not to have a God-complex; it represents an end to dreams of omnipotence, a sharing in death and sin. It is so important for all men and women to experience that they are limited and ultimately helpless beings that only in this struggle can something like faith with an existential depth emerge. For to be Christian means to hope in faith, to experience an ultimate basic passivity and helplessness in oneself. Anyone can have expectations on the basis of favourable prognoses, but that is not hope – that is calculation.

2. I shall develop further, I shall grow

This process of further development and growth can be viewed externally and superficially, or inwardly and deeply. I shall use the term 'sloughing off' (like a snake shedding its skin) to denote the external or superficial view: the being remains the same; this is a natural process which changes the skin. The inner view is 'transformation': I remain the same person, but I note changes in myself which are possible only if a person's being is shaken to the depths. Change in one's being is the sign of a valid experience. Among the reports of the experiences of those who are involved in divorces there is also an indication that there are two meanings of 'fascination'. We may say, not quite correctly, that something fascinates us even if we are looking at it in wonder from a distance. But the point about real fascination is that it shakes us. The *tremendum*, what makes us shudder, is part of the *fascinosum*; and only when this happens, in fascination but also on the other hand in suffering, does transformation rather than 'sloughing' take place. And transformation is the precondition of growth. Sloughing only brings a variation or a return of the same thing. Presumably in that case the next relationship fails in the same way, or along the same lines, as the previous one. People should remember that if they expect something from changing places and relationships: wherever one goes, one takes oneself along.

3. My good characteristics and actions will rise again

I grant that this is a half-truth, since my bad characteristics and actions will also rise again. But it is an important half-truth, also in face of defeatism. The fact that I was in a disastrous situation does not deprive the characteristics, attitudes and actions which came about in this situation of their effect. So they will rise again with the working out of guilt and failure, and to this degree one can say that the transformation which then takes place also provides the possibility of turning that part of the guilt which lurks in failure into something like a fortunate guilt, the Latin *felix culpa*.

4. I can be reborn out of repentance

'Repentance' does not mean that I am now in a position to solve all these questions by personalizing or objectifying guilt; repentance can also include the impossibility of answering the question 'Why?' I am relating to *my* share in the guilt, which cannot be completely identified, and in this connection a rebirth is possible, of the kind that, for example, Adalbert Stifter depicted in his story *Brigitta*: the failure of a husband knows that for fifteen years he had driven his wife into solitude, though it was she who left him. He had left a wife who was superficially ugly (to simplify matters – the situation is of course much more complicated) – for a beauty, and for fifteen years his wife had been incapable of forgiving him because of her own violated self-esteem. Both confess their guilt to each other; then follows some nineteenth-century German, the pathos of which makes the remarks somewhat alien to us:

> 'Poor, poor wife,' he said, deeply moved. 'For fifteen years I had to do without you, for fifteen years you were sacrificed.' But she folded her hands and said knowingly, with shining countenance, 'I have failed; forgive me, Stephen, the sin of pride!'

Both have as it were done their share, and only after that does rebirth take place. Everything which is reborn through repentance in this way rises again – that is theological teaching – and it is more than it was before. In this case we have the healing of a marriage, but it need not happen only in this way.

5. Learning to suffer

I can only hint here at an answer to the difficult question of being able to suffer. As Christians we face the difficulty that still faced the older generation: one has to bear suffering, perhaps even beg for it; it is very good to get to know the world as a vale of tears, since in that way one learns to prize eternal salvation all the more. Alongside this there is the view that suffering has to be introduced, integrated: I have to bear it before God, I have to accept it into the positive experiences of my life. Over against that there is a third attitude: I must free myself from sorrow; I must attempt to remove the cause of sorrow as far away as possible, and to detach myself from it.

To bear, to integrate and to get rid of suffering: these are three ways of answering the question of suffering. I do not think that one can say that just one is right and the others wrong. At all events, my view is that if one exclusively believes that one has to get rid of suffering and remove its causes as far as one can, then one succumbs to a 'problem-solving pressure', which nowadays is 'scientific and modern'. If one cannot heal failure, one can also have a right to endure it. However, one cannot develop this enduring, as has so often happened in Christian tradition, into a masochistic desire to understand suffering as a 'cross'. I think that these three perspectives of bearing, accepting into a wider life, and on the other hand getting rid of suffering, fighting against it and removing its causes, must be kept side by side, and each individual must work out their relationship.

One cannot prescribe the same thing for everyone. But all three perspectives are part of mourning: what must I bear, what must I get rid of, what can I integrate? All three questions are part of the learning process of suffering. From a Christian perspective, suffering needs to be brought into solidarity with the cross, not pressed down under the burden of the cross. That is the great difference between the Christian and the Greek world: in the last resort Christianity does not understand suffering and failure as the heroic tragedy of human existence. In face of the tragedy of human existence there is only one right attitude, and that is mourning. But Christianity speaks of the *solidarity* of the cross in which God shows himself as the one who suffers with love, who reveals himself as the one who loves, by taking part in my fate as truly human, and sharing in it, bearing it. Therefore even in Christian learning how to suffer, what predominates is rising above suffering, not pressure under a cross which is wrongly understood as the yoke of Christian existence rather than the help of God, the yoke on our shoulders which we ourselves have fashioned.

6. I experience myself as someone in need of salvation and learn what salvation is really about

What Christian salvation is about has been indicated briefly in that saying quoted by Dorothee Sölle, 'Let my grace be enough for you'. I would like to set another one alongside it. Appropriately, it comes from Jacques Pohier's book *Quand je dis Dieu*: 'Anyone who does not rise up will not rise.' He argues that the Christian appropriation of the idea of resurrection also has something to do with rising up, as in an uprising, a rebellion. Anyone who is not rebellious will not rise. So it is not just a matter of keeping in view the basic passivity of which I have spoken. Of course there is an ultimate Christian passivity: I am in need of salvation, I am on my knees. 'I am thrown face-downwards on the floor.' Anyone who receives in this attitude is letting grace be grace.

But on the other hand there is also a need for rebellion, a need for uprising as a sign that we believe in God's solidarity not only on the cross but also in the resurrection. I am someone in need of salvation and learn what it is really about. Let us look once again at a story in the Bible which has something to tell us. John 4 relates the story of the encounter of Jesus with the Samaritan woman. Jesus says to her: 'You have had five husbands, and the one you have now is not your husband.' One could single this remark out and say that the Johannine Jesus is moralizing to this woman, but that is not the case. Nor does the woman take it like that. She says, 'You're right, you're a prophet if you know that.' What is important? It is important not to judge. Jesus does not approach the woman to condemn her in any way or to offer moral diagnoses, but he says that the time will come when everyone worships God in Jerusalem as in Samaria. All are needy in different ways. He speaks of the general need for salvation and of the possibility of salvation that is offered. He does not say, 'You are a sinner, now be converted. First repent for what you have done and then I will help you. Then you will have a share in the kingdom of God.' Jesus has as it were 'forgotten' morality. Evidently that regularly happened to him when he ate, drank and talked openly and often with sinners. The good news of reconciliation replaces the diagnosis of the law. So there is a new life out of failure.

III. A new life?

1. There are different starting points

First of all, we must become aware of how different the starting points are. It is almost impossible to generalize about a new beginning. Living in a new relationship which makes new claims can be one starting point, and living alone and taking on new responsibilities another. Children of different temperaments and different ages can also affect the situation considerably. Because the starting points are different, the possibilities of new life are different too. Life has very different meanings, depending who is living and experiencing it. Generalized talk about suffering in church is always dubious. Life is not the same, suffering is not the same and failure is not the same.

2. The possibilities are different

A woman may want a new relationship, but this new beginning may not be possible for her. The love story of Tristan and Isolde, especially in the meeting between Isolde of the White Hands and Tristan, gives an exact portrayal in terms of the husband: a new beginning is impossible. The Tristan who after exile and separation from Isolde of the Fair Hair now meets Isolde of the White Hands is psychologically and physically quite incapable of a new life in this respect. The Tristan whose name comes from *tristesse* does not know the lightness of the new joy of love. That is a model for one possible experience.

A second model is that of a woman who does not want a new relationship. She cultivates the art of being alone without projecting the lack of relationship on to her children. A third model is that I become open to a new process of relationships in my life. The possibilities are so different that it is impossible to say what is generally the case, what should usually be advised. Dorothee Sölle shows this clearly in her book *Suffering*: I learn that the new life will take place in solidarity; it is always good if those involved are in solidarity with one another, but I need autonomy, self-determination, to discover where the new life will lead. What I did not learn before the failure is all the more difficult for me in failure.

3. No matter how different the situations are, they have one thing in common: at all events we can live with more awareness, experience life more actively

Bringing life alive simply means making the experience of the intensity of life stronger. Those who really believe, experience hope as meaningful because they can live more intensively with it. If I did not live more intensively through Christian faith, if the experience of Christian faith did not strengthen my feeling for what makes me 'rise higher and sink deeper', as Robert Musil puts it, then this faith would not be empiricism, experience, but mere convention. It is possible to bring life alive where the contrasts are sharper – and in failure the contrasts are indeed sharper.

Bringing life alive and living it with more awareness proves possible where contacts become possible. In many cases new contacts are necessary because of the new beginning in failure: the sole parent with a group to relate to; someone else starting a new job. Here there is a need for the experience of solidarity, above all the solidarity of church communities. If I want to live with more awareness, make life come alive, then I must ultimately attempt to anchor my own identity more deeply; I must try to see what is concealed behind my own identity. Some theological comments can be made about that: about the relationship between 'If I say "I"' and 'If I say "God"'. 'God works, and I become,' said Master Eckhart on this deepening of self-knowledge.

4. New ways of life after failure can create problems with social or institutional norms which I must face

That, too, must be kept in view; to do otherwise is to overlook reality.

Anyone who embarks on a particular course which does not fit in with prevalent norms must expect to come up against misunderstanding or rejection. One example of this is the sanction in the Catholic Church in the case of remarriage after divorce. One cannot act as though there were no such norms – obscure though they may be. That does not mean that they are given once for all and thus unchangeable. But only if one actively challenges them can there be any expectation that in the long run they will be changed. Two things are needed here: first, for those involved to feed in their authentic experiences and thus confront existing norms or doctrines; secondly, for those in their social environment to be ready to listen to the experiences of individuals involved and to begin to question such norms on the basis of these encounters.

5. What sense does my story make to God?

Here I return to my starting point: the central statement of Christian faith about the *image* of God is 'God is love'. First of all we have to see how God himself shows love. To begin with, I said that love is shown in the fact that individuals are worth more before God than they are before themselves or before others. That means that first of all it is important to see that in faith we experience God as love, which means a revaluation for us. Love revalues by going to a person as if he or she were the only person in the world. We accept that God loves each and everyone in the same way and yet each individual specially. That is difficult for us to understand, and we can think of it only as a paradox. The paradox of the love of God, i.e. the love which proceeds from God, is that it is 'for all equally and yet at the same time for each specially'. This is a mystery. But we have analogies for this mystery. It is not by chance that God is called 'father' or 'mother' even before Jesus (e.g. by Hosea), because fatherly and motherly love can in fact accept all children in the same way and yet each one in particular. That is the truly Christian image that we have for God. All in the same way and yet each one in particular – that is a mystery.

Here we also need to remember that this mystery becomes manifest if we live 'no longer in faith but by sight', i.e. with the resurrection. The Last Things show us how preferential love and openness go together. That will become evident only in heaven. Hence the question what sense my story makes to God, the story of my failure, the story of two relationships one after the other, for I have failed in preferential love. And I am someone who cannot offer total openness to all. There are limits to openness, but on the other hand there are also limits to preferential love. That becomes particularly clear in failure: now this life which so involved preferential love has been torn apart. However, I need the preferential love just as much as anyone else, or as I need it from God. In the resurrection it becomes evident, so to speak, how preferential love and universal love belong together. That means the way in which I form a new relationship with people whom I cannot love equally and at the same time in this world. For I must always love someone first and then the others. So my failure and all the good that I nevertheless experienced in the relationship which came to an end are held in the resurrection in such a way that all the good things will rise again: for me, for the others involved, for everyone. That means that I may not allow myself to suppress the Christian hope. For the fact that 'the kingdom of God is at hand' means that in Jesus of Nazareth it should be possible for a bit of this heaven in which preferential love and openness belong together to come about now. So I, too, must attempt to practise it and experience it a little.

The text which Dorothee Sölle prefaces to her book *Suffering* should give us confidence here. It comes from Revelation 21. 'Behold, the tabernacle of God is with men. He will dwell with them and they will be his people. God himself will be with them. And he will wipe away all tears from their eyes, and death will be no more, neither sorrow nor crying, nor pain, for the former things have passed away.'

Translated by John Bowden

Bibliography

D. Sölle, *Suffering*, London 1976
D. Sölle, *Die Hinreise*, Stuttgart 1975
J. Pohier, *Quand je dis Dieu*, Paris 1977
D. Mieth, *Ehe als Entwurf*, Mainz 1984
W. Böhme (ed.), *Liebe – stark wie der Tod*, Herranalber Texte 55, *Lerne leiden*, Herrenalber Texte 67

Coping with Failure, 'Why me?' Opportunities for Learning to Live

Erika Schuchardt

'Eloi, Eloi, lama sabacthani?' – 'My God, my God, why have you forsaken me?' (Jesus' words on the cross, Mark 15.34)

'Abba, Father, all things are possible for you; let this cup pass from me! But not what I will, but what you will' (Jesus' words in Gethsemane, Mark 14.36)

Who am I? They also tell me
I would bear the days of misfortune
equably, smilingly, proudly,
like one accustomed to win.

Am I really all that which other men tell of?
Or am I only what I know of myself,
restless and longing and sick, like a bird in a cage,
trembling with anger at despotisms and petty humiliations,

weary and empty at praying, at thinking, at making,
faint, and ready to say farewell to it all?

Who am I? This or the other?
Am I one person today, and tomorrow another?
Am I both at once? A hypocrite before others,
and before myself a contemptible woebegone weakling?

Who am I? They mock me, these lonely questions of mine.
Whoever I am, thou knowest, O God, I am thine.

(Bonhoeffer's questions from Tegel prison to his friend – 'You are the only one who knows . . .' –, not to his parents, in 1944, the year of his execution)[1]

That Dietrich Bonhoeffer, almost two thousand years after Jesus, can admit and state that he is only in control of himself for part of the time and that he has become someone who no longer knows himself points us towards an important spiritual process. Think of the prophets of the Old Testament, mystics, contemporaries who have impressed us – none can be thought of as being always in control of themselves. The inexpressible – the other being – is seen only by the one who is not under control.

It is this that Sören Kierkegaard develops in his struggle for the 'Either-Or' as the 'new reflection of human beings', as their 'authentic being'. For Kierkegaard there is only the one leap 'a hundred thousand fathoms deep into the abyss', the 'venture of faith', 'entrusting oneself unreservedly to the loving God in the deep threat, the 'uncertainty and insecurity of human existence.'[2] (Soren Kierkegaard, *Either-Or*, 1843)

This is existentially and philosophically the motive force behind the deep questions of Hans Jonas, the suffering, persecuted Jew, presented under the provocative title 'The Concept of God after Auschwitz'. Here he spells out his insights: 'He (God) is not *all*-powerful . . .' 'God is silent. And now I (Jonas) say: he does not intervene, not because he did not want to but because he could not . . .' 'In the mere admission of human freedom there is a renunciation of divine power.' So any 'answer to Job's question' can no longer be a 'stammering before the eternal mystery'. Jonas writes: 'My answer is the opposite of that of the book of Job. That calls on the fullness of the power of the Creator God, mine on his renunciation of power . . . For the renunciation took place in order that we might be. That too, it seems to me, is an answer to Job: that in him God himself suffers.'[3]

However, in personal, confidential conversation even with him – the philosopher – words fail and the inexpressible reveals itself in the all too clear language of tears.' (Hans Jonas, *Der Gottesbegriff nach Auschwitz*, 1984)

Here is the outcry of men and women over two thousand years: 'Why have you forsaken me?' 'Who am I?' 'Who are you, God?' 'Who are you after Auschwitz?'

The steps, the ways, the processes of Christians whose names became known all over the world, all agree with the findings of my investigations:

Even Christians know no way round suffering, though they may well know a way through it – with God. Darkness is not the absence of God but the hiddenness of God, in which we seek him – in his footsteps – and find him again.[4] (Erika Schuchardt, *Why is this happening to me?*)

People constantly ask me, 'Do Christians find it easier to cope with failures and crises?' On the one hand, I must reply emphatically, 'No'. On the basis of years of research and direct involvement in pastoral care I must make it clear that in the hardest times of suffering Christians often have not only to bear their own failure and crisis but also to hang on to their faith and endure temptation. That means that as well as their visible sufferings Christians must also struggle with their image of a God who has so far been little in evidence. The rift through creation now also runs through Christians themselves. Often, now, for the first time in their lives, they have to understand their theology of the cross, their rational knowledge *about* the way of discipleship, existentially and urgently, under the burden of the cross *in* discipleship. Now, inexorably, what they have to learn to bear is no longer just any cross, but their own cross. On the other hand, I must report what almost all the authors of the more than 500 biographies which I have examined express: the Christian has someone to turn to day and night, a hearer, a partner in dialogue. Christians have God, to whom they can turn in trust – as did the classical Job – at any time, in any hour, at any moment, in prayer, accusation, silence, weeping. God is always there, God always listens, and God puts up with all our complaints.

I refer to these questions – as reflected in European and non-European biographies – in my book *Why is this happening to me . . .? Guidance and hope for those who suffer*, which is to appear in English this year. In what follows I want to concentrate on the aspect of dealing with failure, and the opportunities for learning which it gives. I shall approach the issue in two stages:

1. Coping with failure as a learning process (as reflected by 500 life stories);
2. Working through crises as a learning process in the book by the American Nobel prizewinner Pearl S. Buck, *The Child who Never Grew*.

Coping with failure as a learning process, reflected in 500 life stories

For about ten years I was involved in showing how it might be possible to work through crises with the help of the analysis provided by the biographies of handicapped people or those involved. The biographies of the handicapped and those related to them to some degree present ordinary human crises writ large. However, there is one decisive difference: those who are not yet involved, those 'without a handicap', can escape burdensome situations all their lives – often to the time of their death – whereas those affected, the 'handicapped', find it much more difficult to avoid working through their handicap, their crisis, all their lives.

Diagram I **Year of publication and number of biographies**

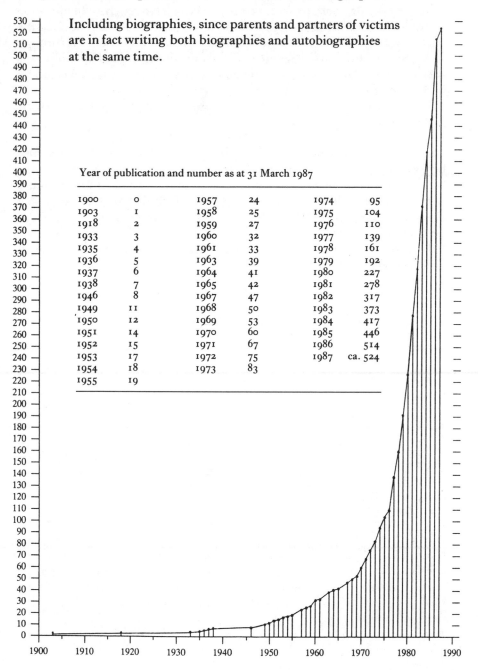

Including biographies, since parents and partners of victims are in fact writing both biographies and autobiographies at the same time.

Year of publication and number as at 31 March 1987

1900	0	1957	24	1974	95
1903	1	1958	25	1975	104
1918	2	1959	27	1976	110
1933	3	1960	32	1977	139
1935	4	1961	33	1978	161
1936	5	1963	39	1979	192
1937	6	1964	41	1980	227
1938	7	1965	42	1981	278
1946	8	1967	47	1982	317
1949	11	1968	50	1983	373
1950	12	1969	53	1984	417
1951	14	1970	60	1985	446
1952	15	1971	67	1986	514
1953	17	1972	75	1987	ca. 524
1954	18	1973	83		
1955	19				

To bring out my thesis of 'working through crises as a learning process', I want to go on to offer some results of my own research. The question 'How do those involved learn to live with their handicap/crisis?' formed the basis of an examination of particular cases: the first approach was through an analysis of more than 500 biographies;[5] this was followed by interviews with contemporaries who were still alive[6] (numbering 131), backed up by verification and group discussion.

Four diagrams are provided to clarify the sample used in the first investigation:

Diagram I indicates the years of publication and quantity of biographies between 1900 and 1987; these include autobiograhies, since both parents and partners of those affected are writing biographies and autobiographies at the same time. The steep rise in the curve from 1970 (of 60 out of 524 biographies) indicates the increasing sensitivity and change in awareness in West Germany to the social relevance of crisis as a challenge to learning.

Diagram II draws attention to the different social and educational backgrounds of the authors of the biographies. It is worth noting that just half (200) are translations into German, particularly from American (89),

Diagram II Social and educational background of the biographers

European countries

	Austria	Denmark	East Germany	France
German	8		26	
Translated		1		39

	Great Britain	Italy	Netherlands	Norway
German				
Translated	45	2	4	4

	Sweden	Switzerland	West Germany
German		9	281
Translated	4	1	

Non-European countries

	Colombia	Israel	Japan	Mexico	USSR	USA
Translated	1	2	1	1	6	89

Total

German	324
Translated	200
	524

English (45) and French (39); there are individual translations from Russian (6), Dutch (4), Norwegian (4), Swedish (4), Italian (2), Hebrew (2), Spanish (2), Danish (2) and Japanese (1).

Diagram III indicates the different kinds of handicaps or disturbances in life from the perspective of which the biographers have written as authors: under the classification 'types of handicap', reports of mental handicap are numerically the most frequent (93); next comes physical handicap (78), then follows in third place loss of the senses, sight and hearing (59); fourth come relatives or companions of the mentally handicapped (46); in fifth and sixth places come those with a speech handicap (11) and learning problems (1). It is not evident from Diagram III that accounts from the chronically sick which fall under the category of 'long-term illnesses', with afflictions like cancer (76), epilepsy (59), multiple sclerosis (9) and others (90), only begin to appear from 1970 onwards and then with increasing frequency; from 1970 the number of these biographies rose rapidly in a period of only seventeen years (1970–1987) to 234 in all, i.e. to just about half of the 524 biographies, as opposed to 290 by people with handicaps. It should be pointed out that the latter were written in a time-span more than five times as long, of 87 years in all (1900–1987).

Diagram III **Biographers and handicaps* or disruptions to life**

	Mental	Physical	Kinds of handicap Learning	Psychological	Sense	Speech
Victims	–	60	–	38	39	7
Parents	35	7	–	12	3	1
Partners	–	–	–	5	1	–
Professional people	11	11	1	38	16	3
	46	78	1	93	59	11

	Cancer	Long-term illness Multiple Sclerosis	Epilepsy	Other	Total
Victims	43	7	50	38	282
Parents	10	–	4	10	82
Partners	12	–	1	8	27
Professional people	12	2	5	34	133
	76	9	59	90	524

*The classification of handicap is that of the Deutscher Bildungsrat, Bonn 1973.

Diagram IV indicates the increasing shift from a one-sided burden on women lasting over a long period towards a more balanced readiness of men and women to help to cope with crisis. In numerically almost the same proportions, in 1987 217 men and 272 women wrote, and there were thirty-five joint works by men and women together. By contrast, more detailed cross-sections bring out the long-lasting problem of a one-sided particular burden, especially on women: even in 1980, women were predominant, reporting in a majority of more than $\frac{4}{5}$; in 1984 this predominance was then reduced to more than $\frac{2}{3}$ until finally in 1987 a balance emerged, with almost the same number of male and female biographers, and there was an increasing tendency towards joint biographies.

Diagram IV **Status of the biographers**

Victims	Women 154	Men 123	Shared 5	Total 282
Parents	Mothers 54	Fathers 21	Shared 7	Total 82
Partners	Female 12	Male 7	Shared 8	Total 27
Professional people	Women 46	Men 62	Shared 9	Total 117
Victims with professional people	Women 6	Men 4	Shared 6	Total 16
	272	217	35	524

In examining the question of working through crises as an opportunity to learn, it would seem helpful to demonstrate the long course of the infinitely difficult process of learning by working through such existential crises. In looking through the biographies it was impressive to note that regardless of what produces the crisis, whether this is physical or psychological, whether it affects the senses or the mind; whether this is chronic illness or the consequences of knowledge of imminent death, the same stages of this learning process must be lived through and overcome by all concerned before a new identity or a social reintegration can be achieved. Given this identity of situation it is important that by analogy those who are not yet affected live through the same learning process if they inevitably find themselves in identity crises like unemployment, loss of a partner, or the intimation of death. Therefore one cannot just call this learning process coping with handicap; it is coping with crisis.

To clarify this learning process of coping with crisis it may be helpful to imagine ourselves being confronted with a diagnosis of terminal illness or cancer, being told 'Your accident will result in paralysis', or 'Your child or grandchild is physically healthy but mentally handicapped', or 'Your child is a drug addict' or 'Your child is doomed to unemployment'. Sooner or later we would be bound to ask ourselves the question 'Why?' But seldom if ever do we allow the opposite question, 'Why not me?' If we dare to attempt to accept the first question, in anticipation we experience the phases of the process of coping which I shall describe as 'spiral phases', in order to justice to the dynamic of this struggle to find identity – a struggle which often lasts a lifetime. The image of the spiral also demonstrates the mutual inter-relationship of the eight spiral phases of the learning process of coping with crisis which can build up layer by layer (though long drawn out from one another), exist side by side in parallel or even overlap. I shall now go on to describe the whole process.

Spiral phase 1: Uncertainty

Initially, at the onset of a crisis or handicap there is shock. What prompts the crisis – an accident, a piece of news, an event – strikes like lightning and destroys a well-ordered life with familiar landmarks. Without preparation the person is confronted with a totally different situation; as the crisis breaks, he or she find themselves in panic anxiety at the unknown. Automatically they resort to a reaction that they have learned: they resist, build up defences, set rational rituals in motion, do everything they possibly can to repress what prompted the crisis. This shocking experience cannot exist because it may not exist. The person affected cannot bear it, and fights for breathing-space by constantly new defence-mechanisms. The main characteristic of all those in this state of confusion following the crisis is that of implicit denial. Kübler-Ross calls this condition of uncertainty 'Not-wanting-to-perceive and isolation'. But 'not-wanting' would be a deliberate process, whereas the term uncertainty indicates that this is a semi-conscious state, a matter of not being able to take things in, with a tendency to deny the crisis. At the level of everyday language this state corresponds to the question 'What's happening . . .?'

It will be clear to those trained in linguistic analysis that behind this question is already the unadmitted thought that a recognition of the crisis is already being latently prepared for. For others involved, it is helpful to describe spiral phase 1 more accurately as the phase of entry or recognition. Three typical intermediate phases can be established in this initial stage: they can either follow one another or exist alongside and with one another and are of varying duration.

Intermediate phase 1.1: Ignorance
'What does it mean?'

Intermediate phase 1.2: Insecurity
'It must mean something.'

Intermediate phase 1.3: Inability to accept
'It must be a mistake.'

In these intermediate phases from uncertainty (1) to certainty (2) there will often already be one or more who know (the partner, the doctor, the neighbour, the fellow patient), as opposed to the person involved, who does not yet know. That changes the climate: those who know have a responsibility; how they behave will set the direction for future relationships, whether these are of trust or mistrust. It is certain that the knowledge of those who are in the know always affects their relationship to a victim who does not know, and that strongly influences the process of recognition, the discovery of truth; it can help it or hinder it.

Spiral phase 2: Certainty
   Though it is already heralded in spiral phase 1, uncertainty, in spiral phase 2 the certainty of the loss of the possibilities of life makes itself felt. This can be sensitively articulated as, 'Yes, but surely that cannot be?' It sounds like a negative affirmation and looks like a continuation of the denial – and it is both!
   Even those who have recognized their crisis have to deny it time and again in order to be able to go on living. Those affected are ready to accept the undiluted truth, but emotionally and in actual fact they go on living on the basis of hoping against all hope that the symptoms will prove to be wrong, a mistake. This ambivalence between an understanding affirmation and a sensitive denial is the basic characteristic of this second phase, of certainty. The ambivalent 'Yes, but . . .?' inserts itself like a buffer, when needed, between victims and their terror at the diagnosis; it gives them some space in which they can get hold of themselves again and make a new start, can go on their way. Nevertheless, since the certainty cannot be argued away, every conversation about the real situation is a help towards explanation because it builds up a link between rational knowledge and the emotional state. The decisive presupposition here is the readiness of the victims: they have to give the signal; they have to be willing to speak and explain: only in this way is it possible for them to discover truth. Through carefully regulated intervention from outside, the truth can be accepted, in the sense that it can be expressed.
   Truth here is not a matter of objectively correct factual information or basic principles, nor is conveying the truth a single act of passing on a piece of self-contained news; it is much more complex. It involves the problem of communication between transmitter and receiver; in other words it is about the medium, the fabric of relationships, the connections between the victims and others (the doctor, professionals, relatives and companions).

Statements like 'You have a terminal illness', 'You have a Down's syndrome child', 'You have a spinal injury which has paralysed you' are not just made in a vacuum. They are made in the context of interpersonal relationships, each time in a different situation. However, it will remain open whether the question is acknowledged rationally by a suppression of feelings through defence mechanisms, or whether the victim is already emotionally in a position to take it. What is the attitude of *both* victim *and* friends and relatives, together, facing the destiny that confronts them? Here it is a matter not least of how much the friends and relatives can take, whether they can communicate in a therapeutic way and whether they themselves have inner stability in the face of a boundary situation. Certainly the victims have a right to the complete truth if they are also able to bear it and cope with it at the moment they hear it.

Spiral phase 3: Aggression
   The primarily 'rationally' cognitive and 'other-directed' phases of uncertainty (1) and still-ambivalent certainty (2) are followed by the 'emotional' and 'undirected' spiral phases of vital outbreaks of feeling in the transitional stage.
   Only now does the intellectual knowledge sink in to the consciousness in such a way as to reach the heart: 'Only now am I aware of it'. Hurt and shattered to the core, the victim cries out, 'Why me?' The torment of this consciousness is overwhelmed with such turbulent feelings that the victim will either feel suffocated by it, or – in the worst instance – will lash out at those around because of it. This volcanic protest can most aptly be described as aggression (3). The tragic element here is that the real object of the aggression, what provoked the crisis, cannot be grasped or attacked. As a consequence the aggression seeks substitutes: anything that offers itself can be the target. Thus the aggression unloads itself on outsiders without any visible occasion, in all directions and against anything and nothing. Wherever the victim looks, he or she will find occasion to make accusations. Unaware of what they are doing, victims seek relief from the excessive pressure of feelings, so as to be able to act again as freely as possible. But here a new vicious circle begins. I have found nine different patterns for interpreting aggression, two of which should be mentioned here: the 'death-wish', which is described unanimously by all biographers, and the 'suicide' which is practised by no less than two-thirds of the more than five hundred biographers.
   Just as in the phase of uncertainty (1), denial of the crisis is often fortified because those around who are already in the know seek to spare the victim, so in the phase of aggression the protest of the victim, wrongly interpreted if it is seen as an outbreak of personal defensiveness rather than

a matter of letting off steam, can lead to greater defensiveness specifically towards those who are already involved. The individual who is overcome by his or her suffering survives by demonstrating that everyone and everything are allied against him, and in the real situation now feels left in the lurch and isolated.

At this point it becomes particularly clear to what dangers victims are exposed without appropriate guidance: either they suffocate through aggression as passive or active self-destruction, or they sink into the morass of isolation as a result of hostile expressions of those around them; or yet again, because of their internalized control of negative feelings they fall into apathetic resignation. Here we already see the fundamental significance of aggression as an introductory phase to the emotional working out of crises in the course of the learning process as a whole.

Spiral phase 4: Negotiation

The emotional forces set free in aggression press for action. Almost indiscriminately, every conceivable measure is used to get out of the sense of impotence in face of the hopeless situation. An incessant stream of such 'attempts to get rid of it' is produced. Increasingly high stakes are brought into play. There is bargaining and negotiation. Regardless of the economic situation and sense of values of the victim, it is possible to identify two directions which paradoxically often also run parallel because they are undirected; the use of the 'world store of doctors' and 'the search for miracle cures'. Indiscriminate consultations with a variety of doctors, an outlandish capacity to search out the most obscure healer, involving the expenditure of vast amounts of money – often ruining the family – purchase the hope that a postponement of the final diagnosis is possible. At the same kind, all kinds of searches for 'miracles' are undertaken, like pilgrimages to Lourdes – they were made by two-thirds of all the biographers – the saying of masses, the laying on of hands in worship, making vows, giving away all possessions to the church or to humanitarian institutions, promises to enter a monastery or convent or a total change of life, usually on the one condition, 'But if I do that . . .' This undirected emotional spiral phase is to be understood as a last assertion of the self. It is described as negotiation (4). Here, too, we can see how dangerous the way can be if those who have to take it must tread it alone: it can end in a material and spiritual 'sell-out'. Conversely, it is evident how many disappointments can be reduced if in this phase people learn to understand their own reactions and thus deal with them.

Spiral phase 5: Depression

Inevitably, sooner or later, all negotiation in the 'world store of doctors' or the 'search for miracles' is doomed to failure; those severely ill with cancer cannot avoid the certainty of their death; the paralysed victims of accidents can no longer deny the loss of feeling in their limbs. The mother of the Down's syndrome child can no longer overlook its behaviour and appearance. The unemployed can no longer avoid the compassionate looks of those around them. Emotions directed outwards are spent and have given way to a burial of hope directed inwards, which leads to speechlessness. The victims often experience their failure in the previous phases as their own inability; they sink into the abyss of desperation or resignation: 'Why . . . it's all meaningless.' There is a lapse into depression (5), mourning. But mourning and tears are still language; they are signs of experience, of being hurt and of passive resistance in the feeling of a terrible loss. What is now no longer there is now grasped not only rationally but also emotionally. It is deliberately abandoned. But the victims recognize what is still left to them and what can be done with it. Sorrow over what has been lost has so many faces: on the one hand the mourning for the loss, receptive mourning for what has already been given up, a sense of no longer being able to go on, the longing for a healthy child, and on the other hand mourning over what has to be given up in the future, anticipatory mourning; anxiety at the consequences of the loss which threaten in the future; the work-place that can no longer be attended and the loss of social status; the loss of value as partner, husband or wife, the loss of friends, the destruction of ambition. . . Common to both kinds of depression with their experiences of loss and the anticipation of a future diminution of life is the abandonment of unreal hopes, a final farewell to utopias.

Giving up and anxiety about the threat of being given up paves the way to the final renunciation of all attempts to deny the irreparable losses. This is accompanied by an infinite sorrow, so-called mourning: it serves to prepare for the acceptance of destiny, and contains a movement back and inwards, to an encounter with oneself. From this self-discovery develops the freedom to distance oneself from the experience that has been suffered and to shape the necessary next actions oneself. This is the beginning of the final stage.

Spiral phase 6: Acceptance

Characteristic of these turns of the spiral is a conscious experience of limits. Holding out, enduring the phase of fighting against everything in the rational sphere, has exhausted the power to resist. The victims feel empty, almost without a will, but also as it were liberated, on the boundary: they have allowed their understanding to think out all the possibilities in every direction through to the end. They have mourned their loss of past and future in reaction and anticipation. Now they have come to the end, exhausted but as it were redeemed, ready to be open to a new insight. In openness, in being with oneself, as in becoming free from oneself, 'it' grows out of them.

It strikes the victims that they are still there; it comes to them that they are not alone and that they can still use their senses; they are ashamed that they forgot their thought and feelings, their full humanity. A wealth of perceptions, experiences breaks in on them which concentrate themselves in the recognition, 'Now at last I know . . .' I am, I can, I will, I accept myself, now I am living with my individual characteristics. So this phase is termed acceptance (6). I accept myself with my characteristic of paralysis. I accept myself as the mother of a Down's syndrome child. I am not living against but with the crisis. I am a person like everyone else. We all must learn to live with our crisis, our limitations, and we all do so. I want to experience, to learn, my life.

Acceptance does not so much mean resigned surrender as a state of contentment. Acceptance is not assent and affirmation. No one can readily affirm severe losses, but individuals can learn to accept the inevitable in coping with their crises. So there is acceptance in crossing the limits of one's consciousness, which now unexpectedly widen. That makes acceptance possible.

Spiral phase 7: Activity

Making the decision to live with a particular characteristic ultimately releases powers which hitherto were used in the fight against it. This potentiality is an impulse towards action. 'I'll do that . . .' is the spontaneous expression of this shift. Self-directed, and including the full expenditure of rational and emotional capacities, the first steps towards phase 7, activity, begin. The victims recognize that what is decisive is not what one has but what one makes of it. Directly and indirectly, there comes about in the person a regrouping, a restructuring of values and norms on the basis of experiences that have been coped with not outside but within the valid ruling system of norms and values. The levels of norm and value remain the same, but the altered perspective gives them a new structure.

As a result of this, action and thought now change reality itself. The significant thing is that the victims primarily change themselves, and by means of this learning process can become a stimulus to 'change the system' – as a consequence, not an aim. But here change means the possibility of otherness through alternative perspectives of action as the result of a new defining of the person within the limits laid down, by venturing to act independently in them.

Spiral phase 8: Solidarity

If those afflicted with suffering are appropriately guided through the phases described, at some point the wish will grow in to act responsibly by themselves in society. The individual sphere, the changed individual characteristics are now seen in relation to a wider sphere of life. The handicap falls into the background, the social arena comes into consciousness and calls for common action: solidarity (8) is the last stage of the learning process in coping with crises.

'We're acting, we're taking initiatives . . .' That is the expression of success in coping with crises, an appropriate social integration. There can be no doubt, however, that this last phase of the spiral is attained by only a few of the handicapped and indeed only rarely by the non-handicapped.

If one compares the way in which handicapped and the incurably ill cope with crises with the struggle of people in unavoidable existential crises, one can recognize a common characteristic: there is ultimately no solution in the sense of being relieved of the burden. The only possible solution consists in no longer being opposed to, but living with, the apparently unacceptable, as the acceptance of a new task which has different effects and which has to be shaped both individually and in solidarity. In anticipation of all biographies it can be said that this kind of shaping can be experienced as meaning and indeed as happiness. The capacity to shape one's life through active participation in shared life is now 'self-discovery' through 'being different' in the midst of the inappropriate norms of achievement characteristic of our society.

I would like to end this account by drawing attention to the fact that I first depicted this spiral as a pyramid. That was meant to make it clear that a third of the biographers got stuck in the initial stage, a further third remained behind at the transitional stage and only a third – of the more than 500 biographers involved – arrived at the final stage. I think it important to say that this difference is always connected with the presence of someone who guides the learning process. (I have mentioned this in my two books on the social integration of the handicapped mentioned in the notes, giving case studies on mental handicap with Pearl S. Buck, physical handicap with Christy Brown, loss of senses with Helen Keller, and psychological handicap with Clara Park.)

I would also like briefly to make a second point, namely that the phase of aggression occupies a key position, as catharsis. That means that if the spiral phase of aggression is absent from the learning process, tendencies towards non-acceptance and social isolation become evident; conversely, if the spiral phase of aggression is present in the learning process, tendencies towards acceptance and social integration are intensified. Consequently, when aggression is lacking it must be provoked by crisis intervention in order to make possible the learning process towards social integration. (I was able to demonstrate by biographical references how the absence, lack, breaking off, or denial, of the phase of aggression can mean the collapse of the process of learning to cope with crises. It condemns people to psychological handicap – lifelong depression in the case of Käte Keller and her handicap in the senses; resignation in the case of Christa Schlett and her physical handicap; and a refusal to accept in the case of Marjory Shave in her psychological handicap – and conversely, through a therapeutic intervention, the aggression can be triggered and the crisis coped with to the point of social integration, as in the case of Richard D'Ambrosio, with his mental handicap.)

Thus the image of the spiral – see Diagram V – demonstrates both the incompleteness of the internal processes and also the superimposition of various turns in the course of daily life and action with others. The image indicates that this difficult learning process goes on all through life, even when those involved succeed in affirming their straitened lives as being worth living. Here, then, the spiral is not just understood simply in technical terms, but rather as an image for struggling through unrecognizable turns of the circle which do not lead to annihilation, isolation, a sense of meaninglessness in life: it is an image of the 'narrow gate which leads to life' (cf. Matt. 7.14), a way through endless uncertainties which nevertheless gives us some intimation of what we will become (cf. I John 3.2).

Why have I gone so thoroughly into the experiences of those involved? Can the knowledge of the eight spiral phases in learning to cope with crises relieve the situation of the partner who is 'being abandoned', 'excluded from the work process', 'handicapped', 'has cancer' or becomes 'a companion in crisis'?

The discovery of the characteristics of learning to cope with crisis seems to be a universal demand on all of us – whether young or old – to involve ourselves appropriately (i.e. sensitively) in sharing with people in crisis situations. We may be members of a church, helpers in social organizations, pastors or teachers; whatever we are, we need to make ourselves more knowledgeable, more prepared and more capable of learning about our God-given humanity – first of all from ourselves.

From now on we bear within ourselves the experience of the biblical message, 'I am the way!' (not the goal). Martin Luther King's wisdom discloses itself to us: 'There is no way to peace, peace is the way!' Jesus' words in Gethsemane speak to us: 'Abba, Father, all things are possible, remove this cup from me! Yet not what I will but what you will.' That means, though: no, do not remove this cup from me, so that I may become that for which you have created me.

Diagram V **The eight spiral phases of coping with crises as a learning process**

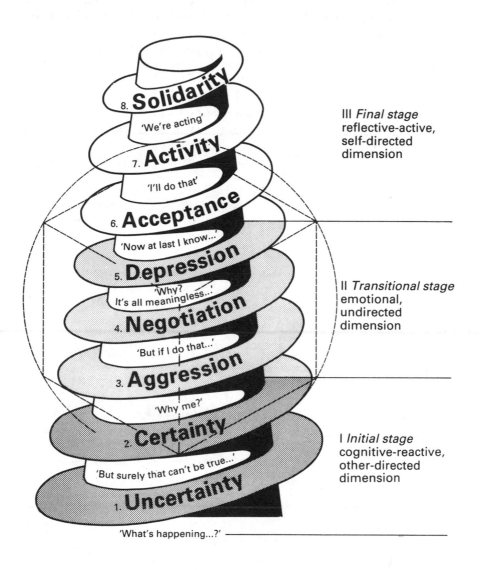

8. **Solidarity**

'We're acting'

7. **Activity**

'I'll do that'

6. **Acceptance**

'Now at last I know...'

5. **Depression**

'Why? It's all meaningless...'

4. **Negotiation**

'But if I do that...'

3. **Aggression**

'Why me?'

2. **Certainty**

'But surely that can't be true...'

1. **Uncertainty**

'What's happening...?'

III *Final stage*
reflective-active,
self-directed
dimension

II *Transitional stage*
emotional,
undirected
dimension

I *Initial stage*
cognitive-reactive,
other-directed
dimension

Coping with crisis as a learning process: in Pearl S. Buck

In what follows I shall depict the phases of coping with crisis which I have described so far from the autobiography of Pearl S. Buck, the mother of a mentally handicapped child whose death ten years later brought on another crisis (cf. *The Child Who Never Grew*, New York 1950).* Pearl S. Buck, the Nobel prizewinner, underwent her crisis like any other mother in a comparable situation. How she coped with her experiences is indicative of almost all the 500 biographers. She reports that the learning process, without any guidance, took more than ten years. Here Pearl S. Buck stands for the majority of women who report how they coped with crisis. As an intellectual she demonstrates how coping with crisis is less a problem of understanding than of the heart: it is a question about one's readiness and capacity to think, to change attitudes and behaviour at the level of relationships.

> It is not easy to learn how to bear this inexorable care. Now that I have learned the task I can look back and recognize the stages. However, it was really hard to clamber through them; every single one seemed insurmountable (41–2).

> But it is interesting for me, and it may at least be quite important for others, to describe how one learns to live with a care which cannot be done away with. That is what I shall be talking about (45–6).

> To say it again: I am talking as one who knows (96).

Thus Pearl S. Buck describes with great narrative skill and the infinite love of a mother the life of her only child, a child that would never grow up. With that she combines her confession that she herself had a hard lesson to learn, '. . . to live with a care which cannot be done away with'. As early as 1952 Pearl Buck distinguished two phases of her 'learning process' which lasted over ten years: the first phase, in which she experienced her own destruction when she had to learn to understand 'the unavoidable knowledge that was forced on me', and the second phase, in which she experienced the 'turn away from herself' in which she accepted her fate as 'given' and recognized that it was 'imposed' on her, for her to shape.

> The first phase of this process was terribly destructive. As I have already said, there was nothing that I enjoyed any longer. All human relationships, everything, became meaningless.

*Translator's note. Unfortunately, it was not possible to get hold of a copy of the original English version of this book within the time available for producing this issue of *Concilium*. Page references are therefore to the German translation, and the passages themselves have been translated back from German.

The degree to which she found the way back to herself by abandoning her mourning is shown by her analysis of her own move towards *acceptance* (6):

> I do not know how or through what the turning point came. It came somehow from within myself . . . (second phase). It was at this time that I learned to distinguish between two kinds of people in the world: those who have made the acquaintance of inescapable grief and those who have not (47).

> It was surprising and sad to learn how many such people there were. . . . This did not comfort me, but it made me realize that others had learned to live with it and that I could, too. I assume that this was the beginning of the turning point (48f.).

So for Pearl S. Buck her 'stages in a learning process' begin with the transitional stage. But if we look more closely at the biographies, we note that in agreement with the more than 500 biographies which I investigated she took more than three years over her process of recognition at the initial stage in order to move from *uncertainty* (1) to *certainty* (2). She writes in bewilderment:

> I believe that I was the last to recognize that something was not right with her. . . . She was three years old when I began to wonder (20).

She then describes how much her discovery of the truth was hindered by the inept behaviour of those around her and through a lack of guidance. So she represents the transition from the intermediate phase of *ignorance* (1.1) to *uncertainty* (1.2) as a restless search for confirmation from friends.

> I asked friends about their children and told them of my new fear about mine. Their replies were comforting – too comforting (21).

Pearl S. Buck gives an apt description of typical expressions of the rule of irrelevance, like 'acting as if' everything were in order; she senses that the words of deceptive comfort were too much.

> They all spoke the empty words of reassurance which well-meaning friends use, and I believed them. Later, when I came to know the whole tragic truth, I asked them whether they really had not known what was up with my child.
> I learned that they indeed had; they had guessed it, and the older ones had even known it, but they had been afraid to tell me (21).

And as a consequence of this common tendency to make light of the crisis, Pearl S. Buck was condemned to remain in the intermediate stage of being *unable to accept* (1.3) until her child was four years old:

> So my child was almost four years old when I myself discovered that her mental development was at a standstill . . . I remained stubborn and unbelieving to the end . . . (22).

> Still, I must have had more anxiety than I was aware of. I remember one day going to a lecture by a visiting American doctor on pre-school children, and what I heard made me realize that something really wasn't right with my child . . . (23).

Only now did she begin to talk to doctors, go to lectures, and finally bring a consultant in, always with the same ambiguous result.

> Something isn't right . . . I don't know what it is. You must go to a consultant (24).

With this *certainty* (2) that 'something is wrong with her', Pearl S. Buck begins her tormenting journey through all the continents, the phase of *negotiation* (4) in the world store of medical knowledge, in order to buy hope:

> Then began the long journey which parents of such children know so well. Since then I have talked with many people, and it's always the same. Driven by the conviction that there had to be someone, somewhere, who could heal, we took our children all over the world in search of someone who could help us (26f.).

She depicts the end of the journey, when the inescapable truth was shown to her in a single moment.

> The end of the journey came in Rochester, Minnesota. We had finally been sent to the Mayo Clinic (31).

> And then came the moment for which I must be grateful as long as I live . . .

> I have to thank the person who came out of an empty room just as I was going past . . . He came out almost furtively and gestured that I should follow him into the empty room.
>   With an almost brusque voice, looking straight into my eyes, he began to speak in his broken English. 'Did he say that your child could be cured?'
>   'Listen to what I tell you,' he ordered.

'I tell you that your child will never be normal. Don't deceive yourself. You will destroy your life and make your family beggars unless you give up hope and look truth in the face. She will never be cured. Can you hear me?' . . .

'I'm telling you the truth for your own good' (34f.).

As an expression of her sheer desperation at this 'brutal communication of the truth' – by then the child was five years old and the chances of a 'measured discovery of the truth' had been spoilt by the circumstances – *aggression* (3) expressed as a death wish against the child becomes quite understandable:

Death would have been far easier to bear, since death is final; what was, is no longer. How often the cry was torn from my heart that it would be better if my child died. This may be disturbing to those of you who do not know this kind of thing, but not to those who have had the same experience. I would have welcomed death for my child, for then it would have been safe for ever (42).

She then openly elaborates on that.

For the sake of others who have to tread the same stony way, I have to say that my inner rebellion lasted for years . . . Reason and a sense of duty cannot always have the upper hand when the heart is broken (45).

Pearl Buck reflects on the periods of *depression* (5) as the first phase of her 'learning process'. It should also be pointed out that she herself describes the experience of both forms of depression – anticipatory and receptive: anticipatory depression as mourning over the uncertain future of the child whose future fate will be to be given up by others, and receptive depression as mourning over a brilliant life that has already been given up, over retreat into isolation:

I faced two problems, and both seemed to me to be intolerable.

The first was the question of her future . . . (38), and in addition there was a second, the problem of my own life in misery. All splendour has departed from life, all pride in being a parent; one has the feeling that one's own life has in fact been cut off in that of one's child (42).

The 'turning point' towards *acceptance* (6), for which Pearl Buck cannot give a rational explanation, and which marks the beginning of the final stage, has already been presented as a second phase of her learning. She herself describes how intensively and ever newly she, too, experienced the phases of the spiral model.

The first step was to accept the facts . . . But in practice this step had to be taken again and again. I constantly slipped back into the morass . . . For despair had become a morass . . . Just looking at my neighbour's healthy little daughter . . .

And in keeping with the stage of *acceptance* (6), Pearl S. Buck also says:

Only now do I see! I'm again beginning to look forward to what life has to offer . . .
    Books were the first thing . . . flowers . . .
All that began in a kind of wonderment that these things were still there as before, and then with the recognition that what had happened had not in fact changed anything, except myself (50).

In her case, *activity* (7), 'Shall I do that . . .?', on the one hand takes the form of a search for a home which will provide future care for her daughter, and on the other is expressed through an intensive programme of lecturing and explaining to parents and the raising of money for research work. She writes:

That I now knew what I had to do, and could think about it, did not of course heal my inescapable grief, but it helped me to live with it . . .

Finally we experience *solidarity* (8): 'We're acting . . .', not least in the writing and publishing of her autobiography, which stands out from many others by its truthfulness. In this way the author builds up a relationship with her readers:

It will not be easy to tell the truth in all things, but to tell anything else would be useless (14).

Thus Pearl S. Buck shows solidarity with all who are affected as she was, and provides company for them along the way: from the death-wish though affirmation, to action in shared, never-ending learning. She concludes:

One has to bear suffering, to know that suffering which one takes wholly upon oneself bears its own gifts. For suffering has a special alchemy. It can be transformed into wisdom which may not bring joy, but does bring inner happiness (8).

Thus Pearl S. Buck, despite the possibility of failure, ventures to continue to bear her suffering and in so doing experiences her crisis as a chance to learn. We recognize that we are dependent on one another if life, and that means more than survival, is to succeed. The interactive model of coping with crises can contribute to this as an open process of learning by giving didactic and methodical stimuli to crisis prevention and crisis intervention, thus creating the presuppositions for a conception of life-long further development: 'Not just to give years to life, but to give life, experience, to years' is a prophecy which in another form was expressed centuries before our time by thinkers like Hippocrates, Plato, Cicero and Galen of Pergamon: 'Never cease to begin, never begin to cease!'

Translated by John Bowden

Notes

1. Dietrich Bonhoeffer, *Letters and Papers from Prison*, London and New York 1971, 348.
2. Sören Kierkegaard, *Either-Or*, 20 February 1843.
3. Hans Jonas, *Der Gottesbegriff nach Auschwitz*, Tübingen 1984, 39, 41, 43, 49.
4. Erika Schuchardt, *Why is this happening to me? Guidance and hope for those who suffer*, Minneapolis 1990, preface.
5. Erika Schuchardt, *Sozial Integration Behinderter*: Vol. 1, *Biographische Erfahrung und wissenschaftliche Theorie*; Vol. 2, *Weiterbildung als Krisenverarbeitung*, Bad Heilbrunn 1980 (fourth enlarged edition 1990).
6. Erika Schuchardt, *Jede Krise ist ein neuer Anfang. Aus Lebensgeschichten lernen*, Düsseldorf ⁴1990; *Krise als Lernchance. Analyse von Lebensgeschichten*, Düsseldorf 1985.

The Road to Emmaus

Carmen Pérez

'Triumph and disaster, . . . those two imposters'
Rudyard Kipling, 'If'

The road to Emmaus is winding. It twists and turns, narrow and dusty.
The road to Emmaus begins when you're tired: you take it in dejection,
defeated. When dreams die, when your feathers weigh on your shoulders
like lead, when the future looks like the useless past, we set off for
Emmaus. We stumble along blindly. Sadness turns our eyes inward. Step
by step, by inertia, we follow the road.

Eli, Eli, lama sabacthani

The battle was over
and the fighter was dead,
when a man came up to him and said,
'Don't die. I love you so much.'
But the corpse went on dying.
César Vallejo (Masa)

Peru, one million two hundred and eighty-five thousand – and a few –
square kilometres, between latitudes 0° 1′48″ and 18° 0′58.8″ and
longitudes 68° 39′27″ and 81° 10′34.5″ west. Easy to find. Just keep going
down, keep west, as you cross the equator. When you see the Pacific Ocean
and, west a bit, the long cordillera, you're there.

Peru, third largest country of Latin America in area, after Brazil and
Argentina. With these two brothers on the continent it possesses a
geography made for giants: the biggest ocean, the highest lake, the river
with the most water, the biggest rainforest, the biggest desert – in the
world, of course.

Peru. Twenty-two million inhabitants, two-thirds of them scattered
round the country, the other third crowded into Lima, the capital, the City
Which Never Stops Growing.

Peru. Foreign debt twenty thousand and ninety million dollars in 1990.

Minimum subsistence wage: twenty-six dollars at the end of 1989. Basic commodities for a family: four hundred dollars at the same date. Unemployment and under-employment over 50%. Annual inflation forecast between 2500 and 3000%, as the decade died.

Peru. Political violence unleashed by groups in armed rebellion since 1980. The cost in human lives for 1988 was 289 members of the armed forces, 607 members of the insurrectionary groups and 30 civilians, according to Amnesty International's report. On top of that huge material damage in these nine years, and more than a third of the country under a state of emergency.

Crisis? Crisis, but a crisis going on and on. I remember in '79 we were talking about crisis then. We said, There's an economic crisis – imagine, in those days – and that's why everything's so bad and there's nothing to eat. That's why the children started to get ill. That was why we set up the canteen. We saw that it wasn't enough for each family individually to prepare its meal. And we've been at this work ten years. Ten years we mothers have been organizing so that our children and the other children could have something to keep them going. And we're still doing it, day in day out. What's happening now is that the middle classes are in trouble too. Now they're talking about crisis. All the same, whatever it costs them, it costs us ten times as much. We always have it worse. Sometimes you lose heart. You get tired of struggling so much.

In the exact centre of a clear afternoon
a child went to sleep for ever in my arms.
He had light bird-bones:
leather skin and desert covered his skeleton.
He was two years old
and weighed eight months.

Before the open door of the mystery
his eyes shone again in the sunset.
His breath faded
like a flower in May
and another nameless name
was crossed off the long list of debtors.

. . . You get tired. Run home, see to the children, run to the canteen, prepare the food. Did the other shifts turn up? What if the oil hasn't come, what if there's no fish? We lack things, we lack a lot. It's true that we've grown a lot, now there are thousands of canteens and we even have a national committee. But we're short of things. Sometimes the new women don't understand that being at the canteen isn't just about filling your belly. They don't see that it's where they have a space to think and share their problems, to learn like we old leaders learned. Sometimes they just ask stupid questions. And you get tired, fed up. We're human and weak. So many times I've wanted to wash my hands of the whole thing. It's not that you want thanks. We do this because we have to, just like everyone else and because me, for example, I'm a Christian and what sort of Christian would I be if I wasn't able to help in my area, with my people? But you say to yourself: ten years and it's still so difficult to get support. Ten years of scurrying around and still the government won't recognize us, as it ought. They don't accept our proposals – the leaders even went to the Prime Minister to ask for support. But nothing. And then there are still mothers who don't understand. They prefer to go off and die in a corner or do shameful things to earn a living. Oh, it makes you angry. You talk to them and feel you're wasting your breath. Sometimes I just lose heart and want to throw in the towel.

The Jorge Chávez International Airport is usually full. Like any airport in the world, with one difference: there are lots of people leaving and many fewer arriving. The crowds which fill its rooms look vaguely like the human groups which at the beginning of this tortured century packed the quays of Dublin, Naples and Barcelona. These are darker-skinned, and the luxuriant hair and dazzling colours of their clothes are different. On the other hand they have the same anxious look, hearts gnawed by suffering. The same substances form their tears, water and salt; and the broad cloak of goodbyes shouted and murmured, woven this time of the silk Castilians wear in southern climes. Another identical feature is that movement of the hand, the sign inherited and become almost instinctive, which calms the spirit and wards off dangers, two millennia old, the sign of the cross.

Why do the wicked always seem to be all right? It's not right, you know. Just now, it's so clear. All the robberies, nothing but bribery and corruption all over the place. Everyone looks after themselves. There's too much individualism. That's how it is. I've got problems in my job. I'm a good driver, reliable. I've always liked being responsible. I've driven lorries since I was a kid, before I came to live in Lima. I've got the experience. I've done the journey to Chimbote, to Piura. One time I used to bring goods from the sierra, I got to Huánuco, up to the edge of the jungle, up to Tingo María. For some time I've been asking my boss to raise my wages. He refuses. 'We're not making anything,' he says. That's not quite true because I see how the freight charges go up. They follow inflation. I know because I carry the bills for my loads. Last week I was off sick. The boss, not to lose money, gave the lorry to my mate, and he crashed it. I told him, 'That kid's still green, he still has to learn,' but he took no notice. 'It's your fault the lorry crashed,' he said. 'Liar,' I said. It wasn't my fault. I told him straight. If he wants to sack me, let him, but he'd better pay me the legal rate. I'm not going to settle for less. They just want it easy. They have no vision. It makes you not want to work. But I see other people who have a better time. It's not fair. The smart guys have it cushy and the honest worker doesn't see anything for all his efforts.

The house has been left half-built. In the beginning it was just a dream in the heads of peasant migrants who came down to the city in search of a better life. It was designed with more love than science. Its boundaries were drawn as part of a long process: first the land was occupied, then there was a fight to keep it, meetings in big assemblies, leaders commissioned to do lots of administration, hundreds of documents drawn up, thousands of visits to government offices. The house was Plot No. 1, with four rush mats marking its boundaries. It was an iron skeleton, communal work, support from neighbours. We got the blocks almost one by one. The walls went up. The house was Sundays of work. There was a party when the foundations were finished. There was a party when the roof went on and Father came and blessed it, and we put a cross on the roof as they do in Huánuco. It was a party, a house launch, as they say in Huánuco, and all the neighbours celebrated. Now it's incomplete, maimed, disfigured, with one window blocked up with cardboard. Now it's a dream broken off before the end, among rows of hundreds of incomplete houses aging before they've finished being born.

The scene. Lima by night, seen from the Plaza San Martín. In the middle ground you can make out the Avenida Colmena threading its way to the University Park, lined by small mountains of garbage. In the background the silhouette of the hills crowded with shacks. Thin grey mercury light, the whole stage filled with haze. The characters move on right and left and stay still until the spotlight picks them out. Then, slowly, they come forward and say their piece.

The mother: I wanted my children to study. If you don't study, you stay ignorant. Anyone can take advantage of you. I wanted them to have professions. Now it's already looking impossible, it's very sad. I keep after them, pushing them to try to study, at night, whatever. Not to stay like me.

Pupil 1: I read the history books my uncle gave me, but I haven't any other books to read. I only study when I have an exam. I have no facilities for study because the room I study in is used for eating, watching television and at night my younger brothers and sisters sleep there. I don't work, but I help my Dad in the mornings with his job as a street-vendor.

Pupil 2: I don't know methods for studying or reading because they don't teach us any in school. But I study late in the night so I can concentrate, because all my family's asleep. I work selling herb teas in the early mornings. I work because what my mum earns doing washing isn't enough, and on top of that my Dad drinks a lot.

Pupil 3: I study at night school. During the day I work selling newspapers. I just go on the notes the teacher dictates to us in our notebooks; at night school we hardly use textbooks. The problem is that when I want to study I get tired and fall asleep.

The curtains falls. Voice off: 'Curtain?'

You remember that girl who came to visit last summer? So frail, with her long hair, remember? She died, she was killed. Seventeen, just think, and she was very keen on her studies. She was my husband's daughter from his first relationship. She lived in Jauja with her mother. They found her dead. My husband had to go to the funeral. No one really knows how she died. They say she had bullet wounds and knife marks. They don't know who it was. Some say the terrorists, others think it was the soldiers. No one knows. People don't tell you the details. They're afraid or they didn't see. Well, you would be. My husband was upset. She was his eldest daughter. People aren't afraid of anything any more. There's no fear of God.

It's ten kilometres from Jerusalem to Emmaus, and vice versa. The road goes in two directions, though at first sight you don't notice. Half way along there's an inn. Nothing exotic, just a little hut. The price list includes wine and bread. A pilgrim who keeps his face covered likes to go there. When the day's hot fingers point east, he usually waits at the first kilometre to walk along with the travellers going to Emmaus. He listens to them discreetly, talks to them in a friendly way. He's got a nice voice for when you're tired. It flows like a spring, slakes the thirst. So much so that the sun suddenly finishes its journey and the inn appears in front of the wayfarers. The invitation is given and accepted: it is the moment of truth.

Agape

Perhaps people will one day have happiness. Sorrow will exist only so that happiness may be recognized, lived and turned into a spring of victorious spirit.

José María Arguedas

I thought God had forgotten me. My friends, members of the community, forgive me for talking like this, but that's how I felt. I had a stepfather. I was orphaned very young. I had to bring up my brothers and sisters. I was like a mother to them. I did their washing, I cooked for them, I looked after them. I did it for love, but it's difficult. I'd work and work, day after day. I didn't have anything of my own. I was like rubbish. Like a slave. What could I do? My mother had to work and there wasn't enough money. Then I met my husband. It was as if the Lord had remembered me. I fell in love with him when we were members of a parish youth group and, as you can see, we're still involved with the parish. He is very good. He made me feel a person, as though I'd recently become a human being, as if I'd recently been born.

The woman's name was Teodora. From her youth she had kept the habit of doing her hair in two plaits, which with the years had turned the colour of a cloudy sky. Her customers at the *cebiche* stall she ran in the University Park weren't aware of her having any family. Her neighbours on the hill said that her husband and children had all been killed when their lorry crashed on the Huancayo road. Whatever was the cause, old Teodora only talked for any length of time to the holy pictures she kept on a little altar beside her bed in the mat-walled room which was her home.

The boy had two bits of starry night for eyes, a face as dirty as his shoeshine boy's nails, and a stomach which was never satisfied under the skin and the ribs. The casual friends he played ball with in the park used to encourage him to find an easier way of life. 'Stupid peasant,' they said, 'killing yourself all day.' But he used to reply, 'It takes a man to work rather than pick pockets.' When he'd earned a bit more, especially on feast-days, he'd treat himself to a plate of *cebiche* at Teodora's stall, although he always kept the sweet potato.

The dog was thin, mongrelly and always barking. In the good times he enjoyed the sweet potato his little master kept for him. In the bad times he fended for himself among the mountains of rubbish. He was used to everything. When the boy ran away from the house he lived in with his mother, his stepfather and his brothers and sisters, no one noticed that the dog had gone off as well, because they were inseparable. The mother wanted to look for the child, but the stepfather persuaded her not to. 'He must have gone to Lima to find his father.' 'They say Lima's very big,' retorted the mother, 'and what if he doesn't find him?' 'Whatever happens, it'll make a man of him,' insisted the stepfather. 'Now stop crying.' This conclusive argument ended the discussion. The dog's name summed up the boy's attitude: it was called 'If only'.

The boy never found the father he went to look for, but he learned to survive. One of the first rules he learned was not to get mixed up in what didn't concern him, however terrible the scenes he witnessed. On the afternoon of one Christmas Eve a new gang appeared in the park, 'from somewhere else'. The boy saw the men when they took up strategic positions around old Teodora's booth. He tried to stay out of it as usual, but couldn't. He remembered that she always talked to him kindly and served him more *cebiche* than he paid for. He looked at the woman's eyes, beautiful and isolated in the raging sea of her wrinkles. He shouted to her, 'Watch out, auntie!' Everything happened very fast. Huge hands snatched his shoeshine box from him. The sound of the wood cracking mixed with the old woman's shouts, his own screams and the harsh barks of 'If only' as he shot through the air at the end of a boot. Through the red haze of his own blood the boy made out the policeman who was questioning him: 'Come on, come on. What happened here? Where are your parents? Where do you live?' The deadly question lit up his mind and made his nerves jangle like an electric shock. While he was thinking of a reply, he heard old Teodora, confident and assured: 'Leave him alone, officer. He's my grandson.' And to him: 'Come on, laddie, help me to pick up the stall and let's go home.' Much later the neighbours saw coming up the hill, old Teodora holding him by the hand, a boy dragging a broken shoeshine box. They were both singing. They say a limping dog followed them, wagging its tail. In front of them, under the summer sky wild with stars, the lights gradually came on the hill, like a Christmas garland.

Reverend fathers, mothers, colleagues of the Co-ordinating Committee of Canteens and the Glass of Milk scheme: as a leader it falls to me to speak on this occasion when we are meeting to celebrate this anniversary of our organization. For ten years we mothers have been organizing to relieve the hunger of our people through solidarity. We all know what sacrifices we have had to make in all that time. We know well the difficult situation through which we are passing. Our demands are not listened to. We know in our very flesh how much it is costing us to cope with this crisis. There are many problems. But here we have come together to celebrate. We have come together to share a meal and to have a party, and that's what we're going to do. Everything we have achieved has been the result of unity. If we remain united, if we continue to share our opinions, our work, if we continue united, whatever happens we shall come out on top. That's why we're going to have a party, with music, with fun. They can deprive us of everything except happiness. Happiness cannot be bought or sold. A person who has nothing always has happiness.

I'd been a bit out of things in the community. So much to do. But when they told me about the march for peace I said it was a good idea and went with my community and everyone. I walked and walked and didn't notice anything. When I got home my children looked at my swollen feet and said, 'How did you do all that walking and not feel anything?' Then I realized that the Lord had been with me, and I said it was a miracle and they laughed.

Going back to Jerusalem

Then all the men of the earth surrounded him;
he saw them, the sad corpse,
deeply moved, he slowly sat up,
embraced the first man, and started walking.

César Vallejo (Masa)

It's not easy to reach Emmaus. After the inn it's the way back. If the veiled pilgrim has stopped us on the way, the only thing to do is to go back to the city, to the fray. The journey back goes quickly. We don't see the countryside on either side of the road, smooth and pressing. Our pupils are fixed on their destination, Jerusalem, the bustling city. Jerusalem, the world; Jerusalem, life. Perhaps, after all, Emmaus doesn't exist. Perhaps it's a mistake on the map, a ghost town, a village swallowed up by the desert sand. One thing is certain: no one goes back along the road alone. Returning to Jerusalem you have company. If lots of people go back, the day may come when no one wants to leave Jerusalem.

The province of Quipicanchis, in Cusco, is the seventh poorest in Peru. In it is Ocongate, a towering peak on whose slopes is situated the most famous Quechua sanctuary, that of Christ of K'oyllor Riti, the Lord of the Ice Star. In November the people of Quipicanchis, peasants most of them, came down from the plateaux and streamed down into the valleys to take part in a massive march for peace. The slogan of the march was *Ch'ulla sonqo hina hummakusun Kausaipi Yarkaytawan y auqahkuytawan atipenanchispac*, 'With one heart we shall come together in life to defeat hunger and violence'. The parish of Urcos organized the march, and the priests, in spotless albs and holding high the cross, marched with their people.

The most important thing, sisters and brothers, is where you're trying to get to. I like to have information about your past, provided it doesn't tie you down. I shall listen patiently to the voice of your memories, cleaning the wounds. The most important thing is this moment when we are painfully trying to pick up our lives, stumbling and lifting our bodies from among the broken stones of tomb cities. We need to shake all the dead illusions off our souls. It doesn't mean forgetting, just remembering without pain, even if we have come from the very centre of the lowest circle of hell. I like it when you talk in your languages: it expresses the great collectivity, the average, the small, the personal voice. But each word must be spoken gently, edged with silence and a smile: heads on shoulders, nuzzling close. We mustn't worry about time. The panic of urgency mustn't break the harmony. Everything is urgent, but here and now nothing is urgent, except recognizing one another as we are – crippled and blind, old, half-dead – and sharing the magic of meeting. Afterwards, strengthened, we will be able to slip away, like old forgiven lovers, towards the gates of the third millennium.

Translated by Francis McDonagh

Are Attempts at the Inculturation of Christianity in Africa Failing?

Nazaire Bitoto Abeng

The contact of Africa with the Christian faith is still predominantly associated with colonization and mission by some Western churches. However, the beginnings of the church in North Africa go back to the time of the apostles. North Africa rapidly took on a leading position in the theological, philosophical and literary spheres. Origen, Cyril and Athanasius were outstanding heads of the famous school of Alexandria. Scholars like Cyprian and Tertullian came from the coastal region of North Africa. The works of St Augustine remain an inestimable treasure for the church in the Western world also. The ancient Coptic Church of Egypt, the Church of Ethiopia and the (Greek) Church of the Patriarchate of Alexandria have experiences which are significant for the world church generally.[1] But in the seventh century the Christianization of North Africa (the first phase) was stopped by Islam.

With the arrival of Portuguese Latin Christians after a concordat with the Pope, a new phase of the Christianization of Africa (south of the Sahara: Congo, Angola, Zambia) began (second phase). It reached a climax during the colonial era of the nineteenth century. Since this last, 'third phase', Africa has been termed a 'mission country'. To investigate the question whether attempts at inculturation in Africa are failing, it seemed appropriate to give a brief sketch of this historical background to the Christianization of Africa. Further considerations are dominated by the question of the relationship of the development of the Christianization of Africa to the image of the Catholic Church before and after the Second Vatican Council.

1. The African church before the Second Vatican Council

Of the 'third phase' in particular it is true that the colonization and missionizing of Africa went hand in hand. The French Revolution (1789), which proclaimed freedom, equality and brotherhood, could not prevent the Berlin Conference (1884), in which Africa and its inhabitants was divided up among Western nations. From the beginning colonization and mission followed the principle 'Some are more equal than others.' The 'others', in this case the blacks, were then regarded as peoples without a civilization, without religion, without culture; and the missionaries saw their work as not only seeking riches and comfort in Africa but saving immortal souls, to win them for heaven.

Moreover they felt themselves under an obligation to spread models of society and church, culture and theology, which had developed historically in the West as cultural material for the whole of humanity, as a criterion of universality. For this understanding of mission, it was inconceivable that there should be any assimilation of Christianity to other cultures and religions, any possible point of contact between the gospel and them.

So the missionaries waged open warfare against African customs and social and political structures which did not correspond to the norms of the West. In the social sphere they put the fight against polygamy at the centre of their politics. External religious ceremonies from the everyday world of the blacks like the rites of puberty or the rites associated with the production of medicines or masks of ancestors were banned without any consideration of their social relevance. The associations which came into being as a result of these various rites, and their 'priests' – called magicians or medicine men by the missionaries –, were branded as obstacles to missionary work and similarly contested, as were the minor chieftains who were regarded as supporters of 'magic and rites'.

In order to detach their followers from polygamy and the influence of magicians, the missionaries throughout Africa concentrated on the education of 'Christian' families and associations which were to live together in villages, segregated from the heathen. Within the framework of this aim there was no encounter between African tradition and Christianity. The new Christians were, rather, to become a self-contained force and thus capable of resisting the attractions of the pagan world. These attractions were to be replaced by festivities connected with church associations and church feast-days.[2]

The African churches thus became – in structure and content – copies of their Western models. Christianity was adapted in Africa to the way in which it had developed in Europe, i.e. stamped by Roman law and Western cultures. At best its façade, its 'face', was 'indigenized'.

2. The Second Vatican Council as an introduction to a new era in missionary history

Even before the Vatican Council, individual missionaries and papal documents had called for respect for alien cultures. To give just a couple of examples, in his encyclical *Summi Pontificatus* of 20 October 1939, Pope Pius XII had called for good will and respect towards all customs and usages of other peoples in so far as they did not rest on religious errors.[3] In 1951 the same pope in *Evangelii Praecones* recalled the tradition of the church that the gospel does not destroy what is good, beautiful and estimable among the peoples who accept the gospel.[4]

The Second Vatican Council developed the framework for a new understanding of mission and of the church, taking further the ideas of Pius XII. In relations between the Catholic Church and non-Christian religions, the Council called for the recognition and furthering of the spiritual and moral goods and cultural values which were to be found among the peoples (AG 22) and thus also for the recognition of the possibilities of salvation for the unconverted. The Constitution *Lumen Gentium* was felt by the Africans to be a document which reconciles Christian faith with the African world.

After the process of centralization on Europe which had characterized mission teaching, Vatican II developed a new model of the church which would lead out of the Eurocentric view towards a polycentric church with roots all over the world. Relations between the church of Rome and the other churches, and their common responsibility for the world church, were described with the term 'collegiality'. As Bishop of Rome the Pope is now to guarantee the legitimate cultural pluriformity of the different local churches (LG 23). Furthermore, evangelization is no longer seen as a privilege of the clergy but rather as a basic overall task of the church as the people of God, which would lead to a new estimation of the laity.

2.1 Inculturation from the perspective of the African church

Acceptance, indeed interiorization, of the alienating values of the rulers in the form of Euro-American Christianity is not only an individual problem for the peoples of Africa but also a social, cultural and political one. Authentic inculturation must therefore be a process of liberation from this Western interpretative model.

Inculturation as the establishment of Christian faith in a particular local church through a dialectic interaction between the gospel and the local people and their culture in their own socio-political context means incarnation of the Christian faith in this culture and this people.

In the dynamic of black African culture there is no division between the sacred and the profane. The worldly is the sphere in which the holy, the hallowed, develops and can be experienced. African symbolism also understands itself as language, as a link between the sacred and the profane. It expresses a drama of life, a struggle between life and death, and human destiny derives its meaning from the victory of life over death. So there is a continuity between human destiny and that of the cosmos, and the rescuing of human beings (the service of salvation) is at the same time the redemption of their environment (service of the world).

2.2 The encounter between Christian faith and the cultures in the Acts of the Apostles

In his investigation 'The Church of the Apostles: A Model of Inculturation?'[5], M. Dumais makes it clear that the Jews who were converted to faith in Jesus Christ (the disciples of Jesus, Paul, those converted after the first Pentecost) continued to live according to their Jewish tradition. Because Christianity was thus rooted in the Jewish tradition, it was first seen by many Jews and Romans as one trend of Judaism among several (Pharisees, Sadducees, etc.).

Acts makes it clear that the laws and traditions of Judaism were not binding on the Gentiles (Greeks) who accepted Christian faith. The conversion of the non-Jews, Gentiles or Greeks, led to the first clashes between the Christianity which developed in the Jewish milieu and Hellenistic culture, clashes which were resolved when the Council of Jerusalem adopted the recommendation of James: 'Therefore I think it right not to lay any burdens (Jewish tradition and culture)[6] on the Gentiles who are converted to God; they are only to be instructed to avoid uncleanness through idols (sacrificial meat) and unchastity and not to eat that which has been throttled nor blood' (Acts 15.19–20).

The most important conclusion to be derived from this part of Acts seems to me to be that both in the Jewish and in the Gentile (Hellenistic) milieu the incarnation of the gospel took place within the particular cultures and traditions and through them. The Greeks were led to understand the faith not through the wisdom of the Old Testament but through the Greek poets and philosophers, through traditional Hellenistic religion (Acts 14.15–17; 17.22–31).

Inculturation as the establishment of the gospel in word and action presupposes that the subject has been completely enculturated.[7] Time and again at meetings of the African bishops the demand is made that Africans should be the specific subjects of the incarnation of Christianity in Africa. What has become of this demand and expectation?

3. Are attempts at inculturation in Africa failing?

This question certainly cannot be answered exhaustively within the limits of an article. The positive shift in church history which we owe to Pope John XXIII with his invitation to interpret the signs of the time is a call to the world church – especially to us Africans – thoroughly to investigate all contents and customs, from the family to the state and the church, to see whether they hinder or encourage an authentic – in our case an African – Christianity.

3.1 The structures of the African church as a basic framework for inculturation

If we look at the hierarchical structure of the African church, it seems to be a faithful copy of the structure of the European 'mother church'.

The new ecclesiology of the Second Vatican Council which proclaimed the collegial responsibility of the bishops at the same time introduced the development of national and regional conferences of bishops in Africa and Madagascar. It is, however, worth mentioning that as early as 1961 the bishops of East Africa had founded an association (ITEBEA = International Episcopal Board of Eastern Africa) for joint discussion of the problems of the church of this region. In 1970 this body was expanded into the Association of Episcopal Conferences of East Africa (AMECEA).

In 1972 a continental episcopal conference was founded in Nairobi for the whole of Africa and Madagascar (SECAM = Symposium of Episcopal Conferences of Africa and Madagascar), consisting of three main commissions: the theological-pastoral, social-juridical and the financial-administrative commissions.

The Catholic Church in Africa today has four theological institutes which are regarded as laboratories of theological reflection in Africa, and numerous associations and centres of research. The Association of African Catholic Exegetes, founded by SECAM, the Ecumenical Association of African Theologians (AOTA), founded in 1977, and the Research Centre for African Religions (CERA), reflect the option of the African church for a successful incarnation of the gospel in today's socio-political context of Africa.

What concrete approaches to inculturation can be recognized today in Africa?

3.1.1 The African experience of inculturation

African Christianity has already put down roots in the following spheres:

Liturgy

Any actualization of Jewish–Christian rites is an interpretation of the Christian message from the socio-cultural context of the Jewish people. African rites and symbols should find a place in this actualization, in order to make the Christian message understandable and relevant for Africans.

Since Vatican II, the African churches have therefore been concerned to harmonize Christian liturgy with African symbolism, with African understanding of celebration and life, with African music and art. The liturgical songs and dances in Ndzon-Melen, Yaounde, are still a particular point of attraction for African Christians, who celebrate living eucharistic communion in accordance with their own particular idea of how to celebrate a feast.

After long years of negotiations, in 1986 an agreement was achieved over the Zaire rite between a Zaire episcopal commission and a delegation of the Vatican Congregation for Worship. Though the people of God in Zaire had long begun to raise its voice in praise of God according to this rite, it was a great joy for Cardinal Malula to have lived to experience the official recognition of this living testimony to the inculturation of an African local church to which he had so devoted himself, and its integration into a culturally polycentric world church. The most important elements of this rite include, among other things, public reverence of African ancestors in a Catholic service, the incorporation and hallowing of African religious traditions, and the invitation to the Africans to intercede for the hallowing of their own saints.

The role of the laity in Africa

The power of the clergy, strengthened by the ecclesiology of the Counter-Reformation, in fact reduced the laity to 'children in care'. But the Second Vatican Council sees the laity as equal partners in the building up of the church through baptism and confirmation (LG 33). In the African churches the laity have appropriated this role from the beginning. A pastoral letter of the Angolan bishops reads: '. . .However, it must be pointed out that when the first missionaries arrived in Angola the gospel had already been preached by some Angolans. They had received baptism in Lisbon, and after their return home had proclaimed the faith to their fellow countrymen with great enthusiasm. In fact the first evangelists in Angola were Angolan lay catechists.'[8] This remark applies not only to Angola but to large parts of the African church.

In 1973, within the framework of the lay apostolate, Cardinal Malula developed a pilot project which was implemented two years later when the cardinal entrusted the first eight parishes in his diocese each to a 'mokambi wa paroisse', a lay official.[9] The bakambi (plural of mokambi) are as a rule known to all the families in the neighbourhood. They are fully and completely integrated into the life of the people whom they serve. Cardinal Malula stressed that the mokambi, who exercises all pastoral functions in the parish apart from celebrating the eucharist, is not a replacement for the priest. Quite apart from responding to a pastoral and missionary necessity, the cardinal in this way wanted to give a sign that the responsibility of the lay people in the African church is being taken seriously.

The small Christian communities

In a church which understands itself as *communio*, the service of salvation is a task for all in solidarity and communion. Since the end of the 1960s, Africans have been trying to develop an ecclesiology which takes account of this sense of community by forming small Christian communities. The final statement of a study conference in 1973 of the bishops of AMECEA who were concerned with the future of their church in 1980 and beyond ran: 'Church life must be built on living communities in which everyday life and daily work have their place. There should be quite simple groups whose members maintain true inter-personal relationships and can experience fellowship in both life and work.'[10] The task entrusted to a small Christian community is responsibility for all members in all spheres of life (religion, politics, fieldwork, economy, etc.), so that the dichotomy between gospel and life, faith and culture is increasingly dissolved.

Ecumenism and dialogue

'The Africans have been brought a divided Christianity without being told the reason for this division. Therefore ecumenism in Africa will not stop at discussing disputed questions but will be concerned with collaboration.' This remark by Cardinal Malula in his opening speech at the Plenary Assembly of SECAM in 1987 reflects an attitude shared by many African Christians.

Between 1960 and 1975, ecumenical centres have been established in a number of African countries. The priests' seminary of Tamale, Ghana, is one of these centres in which Protestant pastors and Catholic priests meet regularly to share reflection on pastoral questions and actions. The Ecumenical Association of African Theologians (AOTA) founded in 1977 is at present occupied in developing an African church history as a joint project of the Ecumenical Association of Third World Theologians (EATWOT) for a church history of the Third World.

These examples should not give the impression that the inculturation/incarnation of Christianity in Africa is running completely smoothly. The Western churches, which have fettered the gospel for centuries in 'Western' cultural forms and power structures, find it difficult to recognize the signs of the times in the categories of faith and thus are in danger of nipping the beginnings of inculturation in Africa in the bud.

3.2 Experiences of failure in attempts at inculturation in Africa

Quite a number of African Catholics who got to know the Acts of the Apostles only after the dissemination of the Bible in their mother tongue from the 1970s on have found in it the real biblical basis for their faith, by which both the whole inculturation process of Africans – who today are 'their own missionaries' – and also the relationship of the local African church to the world church is defined, in accordance with the teaching of the Second Vatican Council. Some African churches find attempts at inculturation so far inadequate in comparison to those of the equally young churches of the first century and the promises and impulses of Vatican II. The questions which motivate our people to work for a just and modern Africa – what can we do, how must we live for our Christianity to become a challenge? – largely remain unanswered.

3.2.1 The sects as signs of the failure of the incarnation of the gospel in Africa

As a result of a study conference on the causes of the development and increase of the sects in their country (18–24 April 1988), the bishops from Congo came to the conclusion that the sects offer many answers and solutions to the existential problems and questions of African women and men: famine, drought, fratricidal wars, economic and political crises. Above all, however, they are often better than the great churches at producing an atmosphere of warm fellowship, of encouraging growth and flourishing in community spirit and mutual help. As a further cause of the rapid growth of the sects the bishops identify the various views about the relationship between religion and life, African tradition and Western modernism. In traditional African religions God is seen as the mediator of power, health, riches and protection, as a God who is concerned for the whole of a person and all aspects of earthly life. People do not expect, as in the Christian church, to 'share' in the divine life. J. Bouekassa regards the sects as a sign of the times, since they put down their roots where the official churches hold back: in the sphere of magic, transcendence, reincarnation, witchcraft, healing . . ."[11]

3.2.2 Failure in the relationships between the world church and the local church

Despite the claim that the African Church has become independent, it continues to be supervised to some degree by the Western church. The contradictory nature of this so-called recognition is revealed in the failure of the attempts made by the African church since Vatican II to develop a structural and cultural autonomy corresponding to its social situation. By way of illustration I shall give examples relating to the lay apostolate, the status of priests, marriage and an African council.

Lay apostolate

To a greater degree than the other local churches the church of Africa felt Vatican II to be a pentecostal feast and a source of hope for the African people suffering under the daily tragedy of repression, corruption, exploitation and famine. As this sense of a pentecostal feast revived a sense of community, the church of Africa gave itself the task of gradually restructuring the inherited form of the church, centred on the clergy, which did not really encourage any gifts and responsibility among the laity, so that it became a church calling for and furthering charisms which give each individual a share in the Spirit's gift of revelation for the use of all the rest.[12] The ultimate goal of this option is to restore the Word to the people of God, who for a long time have been virtually kept in tutelage, and make it the active subject of the incarnation of the gospel in the social, cultural and political context of Africa. For Bishop Sarpong of Accra this task consists mainly in summoning the laity to share in decisions and implement them.[13] For the ministerial church that means a de-privatization of the promised gifts, the knowledge and confession which came upon all Christians on the day of Pentecost, and not just upon the clergy in the sequence pope–bishop–priest. But this hope has suffered setbacks.

In evaluating various conferences of the Gaba Institute in preparation for the Roman Synod of Bishops in 1987 on the laity, AFER[14] came to the conclusion that this synod of bishops will discuss the problems of the laity without their being present, with only a few lay people being consulted beforehand, depending on the approval of the local bishops. The ban on preaching reduces the role of the laity (Bakambi) to listening, to mere reaction, and prevents the development of autonomous creativity and ideas.

The status of priests

In order to avoid the structural dependence which ultimately imprisons them in a dehumanizing beggar-mentality through foreign money and foreign personnel, a large part of the African church felt obliged to develop new forms of life to be bearers of the future for Africans, instead of merely keeping the traditional institutions of Africa going and administering them. Though the lay ministry of the Mokambi is no prelude to being ordained priest, Bishop Ndayen from Central Africa sees no reason for continuing to withhold certain priestly activities from married leaders of the community,[15] since indigenization, the actual rooting of the church, is only realized to the degree that the communities live with the means and possibilities which derive from their own circumstances. Here the bishop used the following words:

> To require celibacy from all candidates for the priesthood seems to me to be illegitimate. That is not the gospel. I would prefer it if people were given freedom. While this would not remove the difficulties, which will always remain, I prefer to confront them in an climate of freedom and not in an atmosphere of compulsion.[16]

One example of this is that without jeopardizing unity, customs and privileges of the Coptic rite are now being recognized and respected by Rome. In the election of bishops and priestly status, for example married men can be admitted to the priesthood and the patriarch is appointed not by Rome, but by a synod of bishops. The Catholics in Egypt have seven different rites, divided into Latin and Eastern rites.[17]

Marriage

In keeping with African social structures, values and expectations, marriage is an alliance negotiated by two kinship groups. Marriage consent is a growing communal process of many negotiations, ceremonies, of mutual acquaintance and help which extends over several years. Marriage is made by paying the dowry and is sealed with the birth of a child. The completion of this process gives the marriage its validity and conditions any further official or church form of marriage. The debates on traditional African and Western Christian forms of marriage relate to monogamy and polygamy.

(a) Monogamy. For the Christian church a marriage is valid only if it has been concluded according to existing church law. A constant problem for the pastors of Africa is the question of the integration of those (non-) Christian couples who are accepted by society as man and wife but remain excluded from receiving the sacraments as long as they do not fulfil church regulations in this respect. The research project of the East African Catholic bishops (CROMIA) in 1978 established that the number of church marriages in Africa is extremely low, e.g. only fifteen per cent in Uganda, and that at least half of all Christian married couples would have to be excommunicated on the basis of the regulations of church law.[18] In Ghana in the 1970s, eighty to ninety per cent of members of the Catholic Church could not practise their religion fully because they could not fully observe church marriage law. The results of research by CROMIA supported the recognition of the traditional forms of African marriage. In 1981, at a meeting of SECAM in Cameroun, living together before church marriage was condemned, but at the same time it was largely found socially acceptable.[19]

(*b*) The debates on *polygamy* are as old as the history of mission. The orientation of the Christian churches in Africa goes back to the instructions given by Pope Paul III (1537) and Pius V (1571); according to these a polygamist can receive baptism if from then on he has intercouse only with his first wife or that wife who is baptized with him. But despite Christianization, polygamy has not declined in Africa. An investigation of Pro Mundi Vita on the attitude of Africans to polygamy concluded that 55% of young men and 67% of young women would favour a second wife in cases of infertility. In the 1973 AMECEA planning conference the participants concluded that classical polygamy should meet with more understanding and pastoral help. Polygamy was regarded by some as sinful, by others as an alternative to monogamy.[20] The SECAM meeting in Cameroun already mentioned expressed the view that polygamy was not a hindrance to baptism.

However, the African concerns about pastoral care in marriage were not taken into account in any way in the new Codex of Canon Law, which is still based on Roman law and tailored to a specifically European situation. The ethos rooted in the social and cultural sphere of Africa hardly finds any echo in this legal constitution. Why must the Western family model replace the African model, when ethno-sociological investigations demonstrate that there are at least 250 family models, of which the Western is one?[21] Did the values of the African family – so praised even by foreigners – prove themselves in the Western family model?

The African Council

In 1962, during a Congress in Freiburg, African Catholic students published a declaration in which they called for an African assembly of bishops. After the failure to include African thinking satisfactorily in the resolutions of the Second Vatican Council, the lay people Alioune Diop and Hgango presented their wishes and suggestions for an authentic African Christianity to Paul VI in the name of the Society for African Culture. In 1977 the SAC organized a colloquium in Adijan on the theme 'Black Civilization and the Catholic Church'. The participants resolved on the introduction of a process of reflection which would end up in an African council.

Since the problems of the people of God in Africa, like the traditional African family, polygamy, poverty, famine, dictatorships, apartheid, inculturation, are hardly mentioned either in the Council texts or in the final documents of subsequent synods of bishops,[22] the African bishops (SECAM) and the Catholic theologians of AOTA adopted the plan for the council worked out by the laity.

On the Pope's first visit to Africa, the bishops of Zaire told him of their wish for an African council. They repeated this wish the same year in their *ad limina* visit to Rome. During the 1983 Synod of Bishops the African bishops, led by Cardinal Zoungrana, President of SECAM, discussed the plan for the council and agreed on the term 'African Council' instead of 'African Synod'. The first continental consultation on the 'African Council' took place on 11–12 April in Yaounde, Cameroun. Under the presidency of Bishop Sarpon, President of AOTA and a member of the theological commission of SECAM, this consultation, in which Cardinal Malula took part as well as Catholic theologians of AOTA, was to discuss the plan for the council and make concrete suggestions to the SECAM bishops for the agenda of the council.

What is the explanation of the fact that some Africans who have followed and participated in the planning of an African Council can feel no real delight in the summoning of a Synod of Bishops for Africa and instead have quite mixed feelings?

Without excluding the representatives of the world church, the people of God in Africa wanted on such an occasion to meet by themselves; and if this was to be a synod instead of a council, then it was felt that it should at least be a continental African synod – and not a Roman synod of bishops 'for Africa'. As for the relationship between Rome and the church of Africa, it is important to remove any misunderstanding which could give rise to the suspicion that the local African churches were breaking away from Rome. Those involved in the Yaounde consultation defined the project as follows: 'According to Canon 439.1, this is a regional African council which is to include all SECAM churches. Only after the assent of Rome is the African Council of SECAM to be called.'[23] In an interview with Vatican Radio on 4 May 1983 Archbishop Monsengwo of Zaire stated that there was no reason to fear a break away on the part of the African church, since a council presupposes communion with Rome and the world church.[24]

The Africans were not to take sides for or against Rome. Disputed questions and differences of opinion are part of the tradition of the church, and not a few Africans rightly question the credibility of the church in Western countries, if on the one hand it allows us maturity but on the other hand does not allow us to discuss our problems by ourselves.

As for the question where the synod is to take place, His Holiness Stephanos II Ghattas, the Coptic Patriarch of Alexandria, commented: 'We believe that as an African synod it will not take place in Rome. For if it took place in Rome, people would think that it had been arranged by Rome.'[25]

If the church of the West believes in the Holy Spirit, as we do, it must trust in the creative initiative of the Christian communities of Africa, inspired by this Spirit of God, in which the African wills to become and remain a Christian, 'as the Lord has allowed him, as God's call has come to him' (I Cor. 7.17).

Translated by John Bowden

Notes

1. Alex Chima, 'Glory of Africa in the Universal Church', *The Leader* 28, no. 23, 1986, 4.

2. Cf. *Stern von Afrika*, 1913, 210.

3. Quoted from O. Bimwenyi-Kweshi, in 'Religions Africaines et Christianisme', *Colloque International de Kinshasa*, 9–14 January 1978, 177.

4. Ibid., 178.

5. M. Dumais, 'Die Kirche der Apostel: ein Modell der Inkulturation?', *Inculturation* X, Rome 1987, 1–24.

6. Brackets mine.

7. Enculturation is defined by the American historian Herskovits as a learning progress which enables people to behave as human beings in a particular society by appropriating its world-view and its social heritage.

8. *Internationaler Fidesdienst* 3585, 16 September 1987, 279.

9. The mokambi is responsible for the administration and pastoral activities of his parish; he is married and earns his living by paid work. He receives no money for his work as mokambi. A priest-animator is attached to the mokambi for the celebration of the eucharist and the administration of the sacraments.

10. *Guidelines of the 1973 Plenary Assembly*, AMECEA, Nairobi, p. 10. The bishops from Burkina Faso are attempting to develop a church life which corresponds to the form and structure of the African family.

11. Jacques Bouekassa, 'Sectes au Congo: Causes et pastorale', *Spiritus* 30, no. 115, 1989, 163–76.

12. Cf. I Cor. 7–12.

13. Quoted in F. Lobinger, *Auf eigener Füssen: Kirche in Afrika*, p. 78.

14. 'Synod on the Laity', in AFER 29, 1987, 4, 194–201, 218.

15. Cf. the interview with Bishop Ndayen, *Spiritus* 56, 1974, 144f.

16. Ibid.

17. 'African Synod Notes', in *Leadership* 8, 1989, no. 306.

18. J. Ngenja, 'Die Kirche und die herkömmliche afrikanische Ehe', in *Weisse Väter-Information*.

19. *Lutherische Weltinformation*, 41/81, p. 19.

20. K. R. Höller, 'Das Fünfte Symposium afrikanischer Bischöfe', *Herder Korrespondenz* 9, 1978, 18.

21. The Lome symposium on questions of the lay apostolate, Lome, 15–20 September 1986, in *Actualité Religieuse* 39, 1986, 17–23.

22. Only seventeen lines are devoted to the problem of the local churches of Africa and Asia in the final document of the 1974 synod of bishops. 'What is the point of three week's work if our idea and thoughts hardly find a mention in the closing document?', asked Bishop Rakotondravahatra from Madagascar in disappointment (cf. *Pro Mundi Vita Dossier: Rome et les Eglises Africaines*, nos. 37–38, 1986, 24).

23. Conference documents, Missionswissenschaftliches Institut Missio, Aachen.
24. 'Rome et les Eglises Africaines', in *Pro Mundi Vita Dossiers* no. 34–28, 1989, 43.
25. 'African Synod Notes' (n. 17), 20.

III · Biblical Recollection and Reorientation

Failure in the Lifelong Project of Fidelity

Elisabeth Bleske

Exclusion of those who have failed by the church's doctrine of marriage

If theology allies itself to those who give warnings, who illuminate the shadow sides of a society orientated on success and progress, it cannot avoid looking critically at itself. If it takes as the theme of its commitment denials of failure and the devaluation and exclusion of those who have failed, then first of all it has to tackle the question of its own acceptance and coping with failure, in both theology and the church. This question has long been put to it by outsiders: does not Christian morality *per se* lead to an exclusion of failure and those who have failed?

Since Erich Neumann's criticism of morality,[1] Christian morality and moral theology has continually been criticized as an ethic which asks too much. Its traditional division into 'good' and 'evil' gives rise to the suppression and repression of unwanted impulses and reactions. But as repression does not bring about the avoidance of these impulses, but only a shifting of those which are rejected, this morality fails to achieve its aim. What is excluded by morality is translated into symptoms or reappears in the scapegoats of a society (or those members of a family who have symptoms). An ethic which fails to do justice to the psychological possibilities of human beings must come to grief. Its inadequacy has fatal effects because it not only offers wrong orientations, but burdens the individuals subjected to it with its failure. If ethics fails, it seems that those who fail ethically are guilty.

These problems in traditional morality emerge particularly clearly in the doctrine of marriage in the Catholic Church: the principle of the indissolubility of marriage all too often has a destructive effect in its attempts at protection. If other important interests must be sacrificed to it, the result can be severe psychological or psycho-social disturbances in the family – which are often shifted on to the children. The discrepancy between ethical demand and the possibilities of individuals on whom ethical demands are made is reflected in the figures for divorce: at the moment, in West Germany one in three of all marriages ends in divorce; in the USA the figure is already around half.[2]

The church still puts the burden of the failure on those involved rather than on the ethic, and it still excludes the divorced. Here the exclusion is in practice not just limited to exclusion from the sacraments, which affects the divorced only on remarriage. In group and individual crisis counselling after divorce, time and again there are complaints about the many varieties of discrimination practised as a result. They extend from refusal to admit people to voluntary work in the parish to a refusal to appoint church workers and a ban on calling them. As a result, it is above all those with an attachment to a church (or those who have grown up in a church environment) who after the failure of their marriage often feel not only that they have been left alone to get over their distress but in addition that they have been morally devalued, and as a result they often get involved in additional problems – for the rest of their lives.

The decision of the Catholic Church not to admit remarried divorced persons to the sacraments in order to protect marriage and its indissolubility puts the protection of the principle above the protection of those affected. That becomes clear in the reasons given for this regulation in the apostolic letter *Familiaris Consortio*: here the pope points out that he is aware that there may be innocent parties and individual morally responsible decisions, but nevertheless insists on exclusion from the sacraments in each individual instance, so that 'error and confusion' shall not arise 'among believers in respect of the teaching of the church on the indissolubility of marriage'.[3]

The rule provokes anger, rejection and bitterness not only because its harshness particularly affects those in an existential crisis, but also because it is felt to be in contradiction to the Christian proclamation. The biblical message that those who have failed are accepted and that their failure is overcome in the love of God, whose commandments are given to men and women to protect their integrity, and that this human integrity is absolutely pre-eminent over the law – this message of the God who is a friend of men and women – is not limited by Jesus' 'intensification' of the prohibition against divorce, but is there developed in concrete terms. A legalistic application of this 'saying of the Lord' which is concerned to take legalistic thought *ad absurdum* contradicts its original sense and is untenable exegetically.[4]

Jesus' saying about divorce is on the same lines as his intervention on behalf of those who have been deprived of their rights. In the historical situation it is directed against the religious legal practice of legitimizing the frivolous repudiation of a wife, as a piece of property, with a bill of divorce, and therefore against a formal legalistic understanding which can claim demonstrable guiltlessness so long as the connection between an action and its disastrous consequences cannot be demonstrated by law. Against this it is said that responsibility for fellow human beings goes further than the law. God's law for marriage seeks to be more than an external bond; it seeks to be a mutual liability which is not ended by any legal dispensation.

The biblical saying can still be valid today only if it is applied to this inner significance (which is supra-temporal).[5] Fixed in words, because of its historical land socio-cultural conditioning it cannot be applied to the situation of marriage in the Europe of the twentieth century.

A theology and church praxis which does not take account of this – under the influence of a legalistic morality – fails to see the real causes and the real extent of the problems of marriage today. With its categories of free decision and sinful failure, fidelity and infidelity, it is far removed from the experience of married people of the difficulty, often the impossibility, of realizing their plans, ideals and values among the conflicts and con-tradictory demands of the society in which they live. Such a theory can no longer help to interpret and shape life and leads to injustice and violation, where it finds expression in church sanctions.

Understanding and coping with failure in the life-long project of fidelity

Theology which seeks to contribute to the success of marriage and to overcoming the lack of success must know the conditions of success and failure. Academic moral theology has long understood that it cannot do this all by itself, but depends on receiving knowledge from the humanities and competent people with practical experience in the relevant fields.[6] In the problematical area of marriage it can refer to detailed knowledge of the psychology and sociology of the family and a wide experiential knowledge of individual and family therapy and marriage counselling.

Failure because of excessive demands

1. Sociological aspects

The starting point of the church's view of marriage is that it is possible and meaningful, and indeed the norm, that couples should live together in life-long fidelity. But precisely this is now in question. Alarmed by the rising divorce figures, and seeking the causes, sociologists of the family have pointed to a substantial lack of competence in living a married life and to its structural instability. They describe the present situation of marriage as 'anomic'.[7]

The rapid and extensive social changes since the beginning of industrialization have so essentially changed the conditions, structures and functions of the family and, with them, of marriage, that many of the values, norms, attitudes and patterns of relationship which previously supported marriage are no longer appropriate to the new situation. The socialization in the family of origin – which is still the main instrument of learning for marriage – cannot keep pace with the rapid change. In many cases it still hands on relics of the old values and patterns, which are more of a hindrance than a help in learning to cope properly with present-day tasks and problems. New orientations take time to develop in the present generations of parents and marriages.

Disorientation, uncertainty over behaviour and inappropriate patterns of behaviour make it difficult to develop a tolerable marriage relationship, and become increasingly important as the inner stability of the relationship must nowadays compensate for many kinds of loss of institutional stability.

With increasing separation between home and place of work, the essential shared sphere of experience which previously provided stimuli for shared experiences of learning and similar developments, for mutual perception and formation of values, disappears.

Where the family is no longer a working community with the father as head of the family business, the patriarchal structure of marriage and family, in so far as it still exists, is experienced as a façade with nothing behind it; this leads to the break-up of such families. By contrast, the new model of partnership in marriage still lacks models for social behaviour and is often in contradiction to the norms and patterns of behaviour in a professional sphere which for the most part have a hierarchical structure.

The more the married couple move in different spheres, the more the increasing differentiation of social spheres with their different and often contradictory value-systems and role-expectations intensifies a difference in experiences, developments, interpretations of life and crises in life and as a result often leads to lack of understanding and distancing.

At the same time – as marriages are now lasting substantially longer (with the general extension of life-expectation and the decline of a high mortality rate in childbirth) – far more marriages are exposed to the experience of a number of crises corresponding to individual phases and crises in the life of the partners. The growth of individualization in our society makes it necessary to develop a pattern for one's own life which is often difficult or indeed impossible to combine with partnership.[8]

With the partial detachment of marriage from its connection (in terms of interests and often of work) with family and kin groups, marriage has lost its external support and social involvement; on the other hand, the emotional involvement of the marriage partner has become more important and taken on a new quality through the new ideal of married love. Precisely in this demanding pattern it again often asks too much of many individual marriages. This problem is often intensified by external mechananisms working in opposite directions: thus if structures of work markedly restrict creative contributions by the individual they can subsequently make a loving married relationship, which presupposes creative individual contributions, impossible.

The demands made on the marital partner in various professions (demands on time, the need to keep moving home, etc.) are often irreconcilable in themselves and incapable of being reconciled with the needs of the relationship between the partners and with the family.

Whereas uncertain multifarious and contradictory attitudes make marriage intrinsically fragile, externally its possibilities are often on the one hand narrowly restricted and on the other over-estimated, so that excessive demands are made on it: its new main function, in addition to that of bringing up children, is to provide emotional stability for the marriage partners (or members of the family) to compensate for the destabilization caused by the pressure of competition and alienation in the professional sphere and disintegration and isolation in the social sphere. But the more the structures of a technologically shaped society lead to isolation, psychological instability and emotional disruption, the less the marriage partners have at their disposal resources for providing one another with emotional security.

2. *Psychological aspects*

The instability of marriage, many aspects of which can be demonstrated sociologically, easily leads to excessive psychological demands on individuals in their married lives.

If their marriage is to succeed today, they must do justice to demands which hardly played any role in the marriages of their ancestors:

Demands from the new form of partnership marriage, like shared decision-making and equal rights in the solution of conflicts.

Demands from the new ideal of married love: the necessary experiences of security, of valuing each other, meaning something to each other, of sexual contacts and erotic attraction, are not permanently available, but must be sought and made possible by the partners time and again.

Demands for a readiness to perceive crises in one's relationship with one's partner as necessary processes of development and adaptation and to work on them to change them.

Demands for a readiness on the part of marriage partners to accept each other with their often very different experiences of life, changes and developments, including becoming strangers to each other.

Demands on the capacity of individuals to bear burdens, so as to tolerate over a long period conflicts which are insoluble (or not immediately soluble).

Demands for a capacity for criticism and creativity:

in order to distinguish independently between obsolete and appropriate models and rules for married life and to make choices of forms which are meaningful for one's own relationship;

in order to perceive how a great many conflicts which first of all are experienced as marital or family conflicts in fact go back to socio-pathological influences outside the family;

in order ultimately not to bear these within the family but at the point where they arise.

Demands for a new capacity for partial loyalty, in order to find the right place in the variety of role-understandings, norms and value systems of different spheres of life and work and of the family.

These demands presuppose quite a different personality development from the former system of relationships and norms in the family, which was unitary and largely above contradiction. Whereas at that time above all the capacity for heteronomous learning and fulfilment of norms was presupposed, nowadays married people need a high degree of autonomy and capacity for relationship. Whether – to match the sequence of the phases of a child's development – here we have a far higher, more mature personality development is another matter. But the development is one that can very easily be disturbed,[9] and it again puts considerable demands on the 'good enough mothering'[10] of fathers and mothers:[11]

On their own capacity to give their children confidence-building love and support from the start and at the same time to be able to let them go and on each occasion to encourage the appropriate separation and independence.

On their own well-developed sexual identity, which serves as a model and identification for their child, so that it can find and establish psychologically its identity as girl or boy.

On their own relationship as partners and capacity for relationship, so that their child can master the difficult and often Oedipal task of development – the presupposition of its own relationship to a later partner: so that on the one hand it can experience its attraction to the parent of the opposite sex without anxiety and on the other hand, without having to feel abandoned, can experience the special exclusiveness of the relationship between parents, also with the limits which that puts to its own wishes.

Given the many disruptive factors to which families are exposed today, it is only too understandable that the demanding development of a personality towards autonomy and capacity for relationship can hardly run free of disruption. Hence development is indeed disrupted, and this leads to different forms of typical disturbances of relationship and of marriage which correspond to them; once again they show themselves in the causes and process of divorce.

The triangular relationship can be an example; if it was an occasion for divorce, to begin with it seems paradoxical that it is often enough maintained after the divorce: in different variants, either of an amazingly good understanding with frequent visits or telephone calls, or of an embittered battle (for years, even a whole lifetime) which makes use of all kinds of occasions and intermediaries to maintain the entanglement. In the experience of marriage-counsellors with a psychoanalytical orientation this often presents itself as Oedipal disturbance: as a desperate attempt to repeat a triangulation which was unsuccessful in childhood (to be allowed to be in relationship with father *and* mother in the father–mother–child relationship without one relationship threatening or disturbing the others). The unconscious impulse is aimed at the correction of a defect in development: constantly new attempts (in new role-play) are made to bring a central experience which was lacking in the decisive phase of development, or was undergone with traumas, to a good end.

Further examples have been demonstrated, in the detailed account of them by Fritz Riemann,[12] as a typical pattern of behaviour (schizoid, depressive, compulsive or hysterical) and relational problems on the basis of defects in development in the intentional, oral, anal or phallic (Oedipal) phase. They have been described by G. Wendl-Kempmann in connection with divorce, and their significance for the failure of relationships has been demonstrated.[13]

In the special situation of marriage today the individual's ability or inability to experience and to act quite distinctly from the partner within an intimate relationship has become particularly important. Marriage today, in the seclusion of its private sphere and with its overburdened emotional significance, makes autonomous developments difficult in so far as it favours idealizations of community and illusory expectations of love. It leads in a false direction to the living out of regressive symbiotic wishes for absolute unity and security ('I am part of you') and thus to too narrow a bond between the married couple. This does not produce the longed-for harmony (or does not do so for long), but a distorted perception of the partner, excessive expectations and exceptional disappointments. (One partner is made responsible not only for the other's wishes and their fulfilment, but also for what is not achieved. He or she is 'guilty'.) Divorce is the consequence of too close a bond. 'The disentanglement which has not been achieved at deep levels now leads to harsh separation in the external sphere, to legal divorce.'[4]

But in that case if – perhaps for religious or church motives – divorce has to be avoided at all costs, in many cases there are particularly fatal consequences: the married couple finally get stuck in their development and each fetters the other, which makes their further development stagnate; hatred and/or depression or the disguise of these by a variety of symptoms and illnesses are then the consequence.

On the other hand, the way of divorce and remarriage, which appears of less value or a 'breach of fidelity', can in fact be a bold decision to life and further development: G. Wendl-Kempmann has described this by using two people with a pre-Oedipal fixation as an example. To overcome the disturbance in their development they have to 'go through an Oedipal constellation, a triangular relationship in some form'.[5] Only in this way will they be really capable of marriage.

In normal instances the development towards autonomy is not completed at the beginning of marriage. The capacity to lead a married life permanently and satisfactorily in present circumstances only develops by the overcoming of the problems posed by this form of life. It is impossible to predict at the beginning of a marriage whether the overcoming of the deficiencies in development needed for this is possible with the partner who has been chosen (the choice of partner often has a neurotic motivation!). In a first marriage, often even with therapeutic help, only a first but important stage in this development can be covered, and afterwards a sounder or more mature choice of partner will be possible by building on this, and with the new partner there may be new possibilities of development and a happy marriage over many years.

But it cannot in any way be presupposed that a second marriage will get off to a better start. Statistics show an increased degree of divorce in second marriages in particular.[16] Given the enormous demands made on marriage a number of things are increasingly indispensable:

> marriage preparation as deliberate training which presents the problems and strategies for coping with them;
> expert marriage counselling;

crisis intervention;
and often psychotherapeutic ('development') help.

A contribution towards coping: revision of an obsolete concept

After what has been said so far, the theological focus of the theme 'failing in the lifelong project of fidelity' can no longer be on the question how those who have failed are to be supported in overcoming their failure. The weight would then again lie with individual failure and how to cope with it. But the question can no longer be put in this way, since it already contains a false judgment.

Naturally we should be well aware of the painful experience of the divorced and their families, and some aspects must not be swept into the background – even in the tasks of theology and the church:

> The experience of how dramatic and how injurious separations and divorces can be: the number of suicides, accidents (which may be suicidal) and the incidence of fatal illnesses following divorces is terrifyingly high.[17]

> The experience of how often (and often irrevocably) the divorced and their children are thrown off the rails: the consequences of divorce range from a decline in professional or academic achievements, through all forms of social decline (lower chances of education, loss of job etc.), through social disintegration to homelessness.

> The experience of how long it takes and how hard it is to cope with mentally: this is comparable to the process of mourning and getting over the death of a close relative, but often even more difficult, since the finality can be denied longer. Divorces that people have not been able to cope with then damage the next marriage and relationships with the partner and the marriages of children.

Church marriage counsellors also experience how much help people need in the process of separation. As our society gives them little scope for mourning, they are often dependent on encouragement and support so that they do not have to bury anger, grief and self-doubt in themselves but can take the healing course of the process of mourning which is needed so that traumatic experiences do not lead to permanent damage either among adults or among children, and these can find new orientations and goals.

This task is perceived in the sphere of church counselling and increasingly also in other pastoral ministries.[18] Within the church, in fact, there are many places where there is an increasing pastoral-psychological interest in the human needs which are often neglected in the social sphere. At the same time, however, there is a danger that the present authoritative shift in emphasis by the church *magisterium* towards dogma and catechesis may devalue the significance of experiential experience and in the near future nip much of this humane development in the bud.

As a consequence of what has been said so far, a new understanding is the most important condition if theology and the church are to cope with the theme of divorce.

The failure of marriage as a 'lifelong project of fidelity' is often conditioned by conceptuality. Coping with it must therefore begin with the concept of marriage and not with divorce. The church doctrine of marriage which has grown up through history must be revised in accordance with the historical developments in marriage. In the light of a biblical understanding there is nothing against such an adaptation to new circumstances: this was already happening at the time when the New Testament was being written down, and can be established by a comparison of the New Testament writings – as long as the original Christian (biblical) intention is not lost.[19]

Marriage as a covenant of lifelong love and fidelity is a goal of Christian ethics. As an answer to the longing of human beings and their need for supportive relationships on which they can rely, like a promise, it is the promise that love between wife and husband can be as reliable as the love of Christ for his church (Eph. 5.22–33) and an encouragement to risk sharing a love on which both can rely and which never irresponsibly puts at risk the total well-being of one's partner. This aim cannot be turned into a demand for a lifelong bond as a binding norm if its fulfilment cannot be guaranteed, for Christian ethics presupposes the feasibility of moral action. It is always our faith that we do not have to obey just any norms – of some arbitrary kind – but that salvation and being accepted in love is given to us first as a basis on which we *can* act.[20]

A new understanding of Christian marriage will see 'the lifelong project of fidelity' as an aim which cannot be achieved by many people right away (their first binding intimate relationship); for some people it may never be attainable because of their psychological make-up and external circumstances. To judge these people and their relationships *a priori* as failures does not do them justice. As a discouraging misjudgment it hinders them in overcoming separations and in the search for and shaping of whatever form of living is possible for them. It devalues the responsible action of those who, acknowledging the limitations of their personal resources, cover certain stretches of life as best they can and in this way achieve their goal.

A new understanding of Christian marriage can no longer identify divorce with failure, and will see the possibility of remarriage after divorce as an acceptable possibility for Christians. The promise of fidelity is not fulfilled by sticking to a commitment established at one time, but in active concern for a loving relationship for one's partner. If this can no longer be maintained, it can also find its fulfilment acting particularly responsibly over a divorce which lovingly keeps open the present and future possibilities of both partners and their children. In this new understanding, pre-marital and marital-like living-together, and indeed similar relationships with homosexual partners, are seen as possible ways of living a morally respons-ible life in keeping with a personal situation.

In the conditions of a technocratic society the individual is so endangered – psychologically, and therefore also physically and socially – that a couple cannot ethically be required to give up a protective relationship. It can no longer be claimed that in principle it is morally good and essential – regardless of what has gone before – to renounce close, indeed intimate and emotionally significant, binding and reliable relationships which, like a family, provide reciprocal balance, protection and mutual support and can further personal development (as opposed to stagnation through isolation).[21] If the church wants to show that it is a healing community, then just as previously the protection of marriage was its concern, now it must support people whose most important relationship has come to an end and those who are in search of a new beginning and a new basis for such a scope for living.

Translated by John Bowden

Notes

1. E. Neumann, *Tiefenpsychologie und neue Ethik*, Munich [3]1973.
2. E. Beck-Gernsheim, 'Von der Liebe zur Beziehung? Veränderungen im Verhältnis von Mann und Frau in der individualisierten Gesellschaft: Sociale Welt', *Zeitschrift für soziologisch-wissenschaftliche Forschung und Praxis*, Sonderband 4, 1986, 209–33:209.
3. John Paul II, *Familiaris Consortio* (1981), nos. 83, 84.
4. See the interpretations of the text of Mark 10.2–12 in: H. Baltensweiler, *Die Ehe im Neuen Testament*, Zurich 1967; H. Greeven, 'Ehe nach dem Neuen Testament', in id. and J. Ratzinger et al., *Theologie der Ehe*, Regensburg 1969, 37–79; R. Oesch, 'Die neutestamentliche Weisung für die Ehe', *Bibel und Leben* 9, 1968, 208–21; R. Schnack-enburg, 'Die Ehe nach der Weisung Jesus und dem Verstänhis der Urkirche', in F. Heinrich and V. Eid (eds.), *Ehe und Ehescheidung*, Munich 1972, 11–34.
5. For the distinction between time-conditioned demand and 'model-type' in-tentional statements see J. Blank, 'New Testament Morality and Modern Moral Theology', *Concilium* 5.3, May 1967, 6–12: 11.
6. F. Böckle, 'Werte und Normenbegrunden', in *Christlicher Glaube in moderne Gesellschaft*, ed. Böckle et al, Freiburg 1981, 37–89; J. Gründel, *Normen im Wandel*, Munich 1980; W. Korff, *Theologische Ethik*, Freiburg 1975.

7. H. P. Dreitzel, *Die gesellschaftlichen Leiden und die Leiden der Gesellschaft*, Stuttgart 1968, 80. For a detailed bibliography and description of this and what follows see E. Bleske, *Konfliktfeld Ehe und christliche Ethik*, Munich, 1981, 15–51.

8. Beck-Gernsheim, 'Von der Liebe' (n. 2).

9. O. Wendl-Kempmann and P. Wendl, *Partnerkrisen und Scheidung*, Munich 1986, 26.

10. D. W. Winnicott, *The Child, the Family and the Outside World*, London 1962.

11. W. Mertens, *Psychoanalyse*, Stuttgart 1981, 35–127; D. Ohlmeier (ed.), *Psychoanalytische Entwicklungspsychologie*, Freiburg 1973.

12. F. Riemann, *Grundformen der Angst*, Munich [12]1977.

13. Wendl-Kempmann, *Partnerkrisen* (n. 9), 26.

14. Ibid., 32.

15. Ibid., 7.

16. Beck-Gernsheim, 'Von der Liebe' (n. 2), 209.

17. H. H. Siewert, *Scheidung – Wege zur Bewältigung*, Munich 1983.

18. V. Eckert and I. Weiss, 'Aufarbeiten von Trennung und Scheidung', in Katholische Bundesarbeitsgemeinschaft für Beratung, *Rat in ratloser Zeit*, Freiburg 1986, 206–20.

19. For a detailed account see Bleske, *Konfliktfeld Ehe* (n. 7), 180–201.

20. Ibid., 180–2.

21. In this connection B. Häring speaks of a 'basic human right to marriage', in id, *Ausweglos? Zur Pastoral bei Scheidung und Wiederverheiratung*, Freiburg 1989, 64f.

'Lord, why have you done evil to this people?'

Lamentation before God and accusation against God in the experience of failure

Jürgen Ebach

I

In contrast to the dominant pattern of the history of Christian piety, the Bible contains not only praise of God but lamentation before God and even accusation of God. The 'Why?' and 'How long?' in the face of the experiences of failure are addressed in one direction in the Bible: to the same God to whom praise and thanksgiving are given for creation and preservation. The biblical book in which lamentation before God becomes vigorous accusation is the book of Job. And before the various aspects of 'Job's problem' are discussed specifically in theological, philosophical and literary terms,[1] it is also evident that in other passages of the Bible, too, the experience of failure can become question, lamentation and accusation before God. So the basis of the following considerations will be neither the book of Job nor the psalms of lamentation but a complex of texts in which it might not immediately be expected: in the Exodus story.

The biblical Exodus story is also a story of failure. As often, the story of liberation gets stuck and seems to have ended before it is properly begun. Moses, the rescuer, first has to be rescued himself (Ex. 2.1–10); Moses, the 'terrorist', has to flee because those for whom he performs his violent act of vengeance refuse to show solidarity with him (2.11–14). Moses, who is called by God, is attacked in a life-and-death struggle by the same God (4.24–26). Here it is not just the case that the tension is heightened by a series of delays or that the ultimate happy ending is made all the clearer by a number of dangers to it. This kind of story-telling is also about the experience that the supreme danger occurs precisely when that is at stake.

But here perhaps above all we have the life-story of the people and its members in the web of success *and* failure, rescue *and* violence, as one history. That even the greatest figures of Israel are 'flawed heroes' is woven into the salvation history of the people. If failure and disaster remain failure and disaster and nevertheless are to be understood as part of the one history brought about by God, how can any one react to God over the failure otherwise than by question, lamentation and accusation?

II

In Exodus 5, in the middle of the story of the exodus of Israel from slavery, such an accusation is formulated against God. At the command of and in the name of God Moses had called on Pharaoh to let the people go (5.1ff.). Pharaoh reacted by 'increasing the quota' (the slaves have to make the same number of bricks in considerably more difficult circumstances). The attempt at liberation went into reverse and the situation was more oppressive than before:

'Then Moses turned again to the Lord and said, "O Lord, why have you done evil to this people? Why did you ever send me? For since I came to Pharaoh to speak in your name, he has done evil to this people, and you have not delivered your people at all"' (Ex. 5.22f.). This undisguised reproach to YHWH comes in the Exodus story between the epiphany of God and call of Moses in Ex. 3 and a further epiphany of God in Ex. 6.[2] A nadir has been reached in the sequence of events between Israel's slavery and the exodus. The words of Moses are a reaction to the failure.

The biblical narrative depicts the failure on different levels, which are interconnected in both content and language. The failure of the liberation is depicted in the actions of Pharaoh, in those of the overseers (in the double role of representatives and opponents of the people) and finally in the role of Moses himself.[3] However, Moses identifies the failure explicitly as a failure of the divine plan. In so doing he goes beyond a mere contrast between the harsh attitude of Pharaoh and what seems first to be a failure of the divine plan. The double use of the root 'evil, act evilly' (Hebrew r^ς, $r^{\varsigma\varsigma}$), which moreover picks up the 'evil situation' (r^ς) in which according to 5.19 the overseers saw themselves, make Pharaoh's and God's action one event. At the same time the reproach of the overseers to Pharaoh (5.15) resembles that of Moses to God (5.22). In the words of Moses to YHWH, Pharaoh's evil action becomes God's evil action. So the experience of human beings that plans fail and hopes go to ruin becomes an experience with and question to God. In this way and only in this way an empirical and psychological problem becomes a theological one. But may one talk before God in this way? Those who are terrified at what Moses says must ask themselves a counter-question. For God could be protected from Moses' accusation only at the cost of conceding a course of events which ran independently of God, autonomously, solely according to the rules of the human psyche and the human will to power. By contrast, in 5.22f. in the very words he speaks Moses sees God's action behind and in the apparently hopeless situation, behind and in the dilemma of the overseers, behind and in the hard-heartedness of Pharaoh, precisely because he does not want to excuse God at the expense of God's lack of involvement and impotence.

Anyone who type-casts God as the good God, halves him and ends up in that genre of theodicy which recognizes God's non-existence as ultimately his only excuse. Moses comes to grief on Pharaoh's stubbornness, on the hardening of his heart. Pharaoh acts against YHWH, whom he 'does not know' (5.2). A second level of the narrative has Pharaoh knowing God better. Even before Moses begins to fulfil his commission, God announces Pharaoh's refusal to him (3.19; 4.21). The theme of the hardening of Pharaoh's heart runs through the whole exodus narrative (7.3f., 13, 14, 22; 8.11, 15, 28; 9.7, 12, 35; 10.1, 20, 27; 11.10; 13.15; 14.4, 8, 17). In a number of these passages the stress lies on God's foreknowledge and the announcement of the hardening of his heart. Here we have a clash between two lords. From the beginning, God is superior in knowledge and in the end it proves that the 'firm, strong arm' of God is superior to the 'firm, hard heart' of Pharaoh. But in the perspective of this narrative the actions of God and of Pharaoh continue to be thought of separately. The observations that God not only knows but brings about the hardening of Pharaoh's heart are a different matter. Moses' identification of Pharaoh's action with God's action in his reproach thus corresponds to a perspective of the narrative itself. We now need to think more deeply about this relationship.

The earliest narrative stratum that can be reconstructed[4] does not yet contain the motive of hardening of heart. Its theme is the opposition between serving Pharaoh and serving YHWH; the basic experience is that lords never give up their power without a fight. Later narrative strata build on this experience, repeat it and differentiate it. Behind the depiction of forced labour in Egypt at the time of the story stands the experience of oppression during the time the story is being told, the Israelite monarchy. Behind the plague narrative stands, for example, the experience that governments are only prepared to make concessions under pressure and try to withdraw them as soon as the danger seems over. But here, too, there is the no less topical experience that the 'experts', the magi and soothsayers in Exodus 7ff., claim to have a catastrophe under control as soon and as long as they can imitate one another in their own efforts, failing to note that they are not removing the disaster but doubling it. The hardening of Pharaoh's heart also goes with such features of the story.

Each of the different strata of the text has a specific terminology for expressing the hardening of Pharaoh's heart. The process and act of hardening are denoted by three verbs (each in different modes): *kābed* (basic meaning 'be heavy, important'), *ḥāzaq* ('be hard, strong') and (more rarely) *qāshā* ('be hardened, stiff'). Pharaoh's *heart*, the organ of his understanding and will to understand, is described as being heavy, strong, hard, hardened, rigid. Above all the two more frequent roots *kābed* and *ḥāzaq* do not have any negative connotations. In its more intensive form, *kābed* denotes the honour, the glory of God. And in the Exodus story *ḥāzaq* denotes not only Pharaoh's heart but God's arm, which is already opposed to the power of Pharaoh in Ex. 3.19. The relationship is also fixed in language elsewhere. According to Ex. 14.4, 18, Pharaoh's stubbornness (here *ḥāzaq*) is an occasion for God to show imself in his power, his honour and his glory (*kābed* in the reflexive form). So the same words denote Pharaoh's hardness and God's strength, Pharaoh's lordship and God's glory. God's action and Pharaoh's action are strictly opposed to each other *and* resemble each other.[5] Accordingly, God himself soon appears as the subject of Pharaoh's hardening of heart.

This brief glimpse at the linguistic structure confirms that Moses's accusatory speech, which understands Pharaoh's evil action as God's evil action, cannot be understood as either a psychologically explicable expression of an oppressive situation or (as in the explanation in Midrash Shemot Rabba on 5.22)[6] as audacity which really ought to be punished, and which God forgave because he saw that Moses was interceding so committedly for the people. The formulation in 5.22f. is to be taken seriously as the theological interpretation of an experience. Here to accuse God is not an evasion of personal responsibility or an excuse not to analyse the reasons for the failure (both these factors play a part, but when they do they need psychological rather than theological discussion). Rather, by putting things as he does, Moses is interpreting the experience of failure as an experience with God. The interpretation is at the same time a form of address. God is not an object of discussion but someone to whom a prayer is addressed.

'Hard-heartedness' – a provisional consideration

If Pharaoh's hard-heartedness was behaviour for which he himself was responsible, how then can it then be said that God hardened his heart? If God had hardened Pharaoh's heart, how can Pharaoh be called to account? This logical-ethical dilemma poses problems to interpreters. What is the relationship between divine providence and human responsibility? How do God's lordship and human freedom go together? Instead of offering a discussion of the dogmatic and ethical aspects of this question in theological and philosophical terms (for which there is no room here and for which – above all – I do not have the competence), I shall attempt to compare biblical talk of hardening the heart with contemporary models of experience and interpretation.

In his commentary on Exodus[7] the Jewish exegete Umberto Cassuto explains that the narrative is not concerned with raising or solving any philosophical problems. Rather, the statements that Pharaoh's heart was hardened and that God had hardened it are synonymous, though of course God's action is recognized behind all that happens. But is this explanation enough when we see that the motive of hardening appears in the additional comments on and reflective expansions to the narrativ(es)? Here the statements about Pharaoh himself and about God as the one who does the hardening stand side by side. Is this unexplained juxtaposition of two approaches a capitulation to a theological dilemma? Do the biblical levels of experience and interpretation stand up to present experiences and interpretations? Or must we not ask on the contrary whether the modern postulate of human free will stands up to the reality contained in the biblical narrative? Not least, we have to ask whether present experiences and interpretations confirm this postulate. What does it mean in the face of the historical, economic, psychological, cultural and indeed genetic conditioning of human beings which is becoming increasingly clear in the most varied academic disciplines?

With good reason, despite and precisely because of this manifold variety of conditioning (and indeed possibly in the face of it) we have to hold firm to the freedom and responsibility of human beings as a *postulate*. To people caught between the postulate of human responsibility and an analysis of what has made us what we are and what we do, 'hardening of heart' proves to be a surprisingly appropriate analytical category. The statement about the hardening of Pharaoh's heart resists the alternatives 'self-caused or conditioned', 'active *or* passive'. There is no conceptual deficiency here, but lack of sharpness which is analytically necessary. The hardening of Pharaoh's heart does not simply mean that Pharaoh *does not* want Israel's liberation; it also means that Pharaoh *cannot* want Israel's liberation. Pharaoh both *is* a person and *has* a role. His role distorts his capacity for perception, makes the one supposed to be master the servant of his function and the actor the prisoner of his ideology. The hardness of his heart is the expression of his consistent involvement in the role that has been given him.

How can one judge Pharaoh's action? It soon emerges that a moralistic evaluation is not enough (as if slave-owners, those in power, those who exploit relationships of power, were simply evil men . . .). But only to refer to the autonomies of structures and overriding determinations is just as inadequate (as if there were no way of changing those structures). Beyond the alternative of moralism and system theory, the category of hardening of heart includes conduct and its determination, the will and its conditioning, freedom and its limitations. To do what is hostile to life (and nowadays, equally, to fail to do what is necessary), which is a characteristic of people of the First World, is to act or fail to act against our better knowledge. We know that our conduct towards the poor countries of the earth and towards the earth and its resources must not go on like this, and indeed in the long run cannot go on like this – but it does go on. This 'going on like this' is the expression of many kinds of hardening of the heart. To harden the heart is to act against our better judgment, false knowledge when we could know better. Now everything depends on our not confusing the analytical category of hardening the heart with the acceptance that things are now as they are. Talk of hardening the heart describes a problem and does not take the description as a solution. In its obscurity and modesty it helps us to *ask* instead of getting *answers* before the questions have been put properly.

A further consideration must be added in view of the question raised at the beginning about the accusation of God as a reaction to human failure. In the Exodus story and at other points, the Hebrew Bible describes hardening of the heart as a relationship between human praxis and *God's* action. By contrast, the contemporary variants to which I referred have as their theme human responsibility in its relationship to the *circumstances*. What many people today do not attribute to God – whether through lack of faith or on the contrary, because many pious people are wary about raising the question of God's action given the present state of the world and of human beings because they think it a lack of faith – they attribute to an anonymous destiny: historical, social, economic, cultural, hereditary conditioning – in short, circumstances. The attempt to relieve God of questions and accusations of the kind Moses raises in Ex. 5.22f. has put the anonymous power of fate on the throne. The fear that it cannot be Christian to accuse God has restored *the* norm of paganism: Moira, Fatum, 'circumstances'.

III

The words of Moses in Exodus 5.22f. demonstrate how the whole of reality as God's reality is held to be God's reality. Here Moses' accusation is an expression of faith – which in the Bible means holding fast to God. Moses does not say, 'God, you meant well, but it's not like that.' Moses does not say, 'God, you have a strong arm but Pharaoh's heart is harder.' Moses understands failure as an element of God's action and brings it before God as the only possible one to whom he can address his questions, accusations and laments. Here Moses' own role, his calling and sending, is also in question. So he cannot adopt the attitude of a bystander (any more than later prophets were able to in view of the hardening of Israel).[8] To accuse God is also to hold fast to one's call at the moment of failure. Because Moses does not capitulate to the overwhelming force of circumstances, he brings his failure to God in lament and complaint. Equally important, however, is the renunciation of another possible reaction. By bringing his question, lament and accusation to God, Moses shows that he is not prepared to cover up failure, to reinterpret it, to count it as a predated change to future salvation. Failure remains failure and yet is not accepted as the last word.

The development of the Exodus story shows that the failure which Moses brings before God does not remain the last word. But does that mean that in the end the failure was no failure? Is the violence quenched in the ultimate achievement of the salvation of Israel? Do the lament and accusation of Moses become submerged in the hymn of praise after the miracle at the Red Sea? What about the *praise* of God, given the state of the world? Let us put this question to the end of the exodus story and its rabbinic exegesis. Yahweh's hard arm proves to be ultimately superior to Pharaoh's hard heart. Pharaoh has to let the people of Israel go. But the question to God remains. If God wills liberation, if he keeps his promises and his covenant with the fathers, why must the history of liberation work itself through world history in so bloody a way? Why is freedom not there once and for all? Why must so many plagues come upon Egypt? Must so many Egyptians, must the innocent Egyptian firstborn die? Is that the praxis of the history of freedom?

There is an empirical-historical answer to these questions which must affirm them. All previous history shows how rarely liberation comes about without a battle, salvation without power. This answer cannot be wiped away by a theological answer. But can it be the final theological answer? The Christian attitude is largely understood to be that all failure, all suffering, all power, belong to God's saving plan and therefore must not only be accepted by believers but accepted gratefully. For what seems contradictory in human eyes is good in God's eyes and by the criterion of his history. Is that the expression of Christian humility? Or is it to confuse the plans of God with what happens at a particular time? In that case, why were not savagery, mass murder and war also to be accepted as the will of God? How can these questions be put to God other than as a lament? Where such questions are not put, or are not put to God, they are either covered over with pious intent, or they become topics for discussion, with God as object.

In the face of these questions, what does it mean that God ultimately proved to be stronger than Pharaoh? Exodus 14 describes and Exodus 15 celebrates the crossing of the sea as the decisive saving act of God. Moses sings a hymn of praise and thanksgiving after the deliverance (15.1). Anyone who has escaped the utmost danger cannot adopt the standpoint of an observer which demonstrates that history has not come out well for everyone. In the situation of the person rescued from violent attack, even the downfall of the persecutor may be greeted with praise and thanksgiving. But the rabbinic interpretation of Ex. 14f. recalls another song, a hymn which according to God's will must not be sung. When Israel went through the sea, Midrash and Talmud add, interpreting and reflecting on the biblical tradition, the angels of God sang a hymn of praise. But God forbade them to sing, saying, 'My legions are in distress – do you want to sing to me?'[9] According to this tradition, at the moment of the crossing of the sea (which – and this too is a remarkable relationship between divine action and human confidence – did not divide when Moses raised his staff, but only when Israel put its feet in the water!), God did not behave like a lord who is certain of the triumphant outcome of his cause, but like someone who goes along with them and as it were trembles with them. There is no place for a hymn in the immediate situation of danger.

This is matched by another feature in the narrative, about the time of prayer. Immediately before the crossing of the sea, Moses speaks words to encourage his murmuring and despairing people in the face of the advancing persecutors. Surprisingly, the biblical narrative continues, 'Then YHWH said to Moses, "What are you crying to me?"' (Ex. 14.15). The encouraging words of Moses are understood as a cry to God. But why does God react reluctantly? The Midrash explains: 'Rabbi Eliezer says: There is a time when one can shorten prayer and a time when one can extend it. Now my children are in need, the sea is closing before them and the enemy is pursuing them, and you keep standing there praying! Tell the children of Israel to get going.'[10]

There is a time when neither hymn nor petition is in place, a time when nothing matters but to set off and put one's feet in the water, a time when even the angel onlookers are to join in, as God himself does. It is worth noting that in the Talmud a further point is added to the story of the angels being forbidden to sing (bSanh 39b; bMeg 10b). In both Talmudic passages the prohibition of the hymn is not related to Israel's danger but to Egypt's downfall: 'The angels wanted to strike up a song, but the Holy One, blessed be he, said to them, "The work of my hands is drowning in the sea, and you want to start up a song?"' (Meg. 10b).

God forbids the song of praise because the deliverance of Israel cannot take place without the downfall of the Egyptians – who are also his creatures.

Why is Israel allowed a hymn of praise which is forbidden to the angels at this point? Here we have the difference between the reaction of those involved and the commentary of the onlookers. Israel gives thanks for its deliverance, not for the death of the Egyptians. But if the angels sang a hymn, they would be praising the event from their perspective, their – theory. There should be no theory in which the death of some is accepted, indeed praised, for the rescue of others. The rescue did not take place without violence – no meta-levels are to be accepted which describe it as good. The contradiction remains fixed in God. In rabbinic interpretation, God himself is the guarantee against the confusion of the world created and sustained by him with a 'world made whole'. God's sorrow at the downfall of the Egyptians, without which Israel could not have been saved, shows that the world as it is is not redeemed. Against familiar Christian patterns of interpretation, according to which what human beings experience as being torn and meaningless is meaningful and good for God, in the biblical narrative and its rabbinic interpretations what is unreconciled and unredeemed is held fast by God himself. The contradiction is not resolved *ad majorem Dei gloriam*, but remains a contradiction in God. The mourning of God becomes a warning to those who still find grounds for praise and thanksgiving in their own experiences.

So Rabbi Eleazar's addition to the story of the prohibition of the hymn in heaven also suggests that God himself does not delight in the downfall of the Egyptians but allows others to do so. The joy of Israel becomes present anew each year at the feast of Passover. But the hymn which the angels do not sing also becomes part of the praxis of remembrance in the days of the feast. Whereas on Seder evenings, when the exodus from Egypt is directly re-enacted, the Hallel Psalms (113–118) are sung in full, on the following days of Passover week only half of them are sung in memory of the death of the Egyptians. The half praise becomes an expression of full faith, once shortly after the direct repetition of the rescue the whole event and thus also the fate of others comes into perspective.

So praise and lament, thanksgiving and accusatory question come together when they are brought together before God. Complaint, indeed accusation, holds firm to God as the one Lord of reality by refusing to address itself to anyone else or to turn into words going out into the void.

This has brought us back to the beginning of our considerations. Where God remains excluded from the perspective of failure, he is diminished. In praise and lament, and still in accusation, God is recognized as the Lord; in neutrality or evasion he is denied. Taking up an idea which Elie Wiesel keeps expressing in his works on remembering Jewish history, the believer can be for and against God, but not without God.

In the accusation before God which goes with praise and thanksgiving, the believer holds fast to two things: that the whole world is God's world, and that the world as it is is not God's world. If praise attests the creation of the world and human beings, lament and the accusation of God insists on the need for the redemption of human beings and the world. The question 'Why?' in prayer becomes the question, 'How long, Lord?'

IV

How does God react to Moses' words of accusation in Ex. 5.22f.? He does not reject Moses; he replies, 'Now you shall see what I will do to Pharaoh; for with a strong hand he will send them out, yes, with a strong hand[11] he will drive them out of his land' (Ex. 6.1). In the text there follows an endorsement of the covenant with the fathers. God's announcement is not just promise for the future. It is the proclamation of the God who revealed his name YHWH to Moses in Ex. 3.14 as 'I am and will be there as the one who am and will be there'. The whole of reality can be brought before the 'I am there' – in praise and thanksgiving, sometimes only as a question, lament and accusation, and sometimes as praise which falls silent in the middle. All that occurs in the Bible and in Israel's listening to the Bible. There is no reality which does not have something to do with God.

Translated by John Bowden

Notes

1. See *Job and the Silence of God, Concilium* 169, 1983; also H.-P. Müller, *Das Hiobproblem*, Erträge der Forschung 84, 1978; J. Ebach, 'Hiob, Hiobbuch', *Theologische Realenzyklopädie* 15, 360–80; id. *Leviathan and Behemoth*, Paderborn 1984.

2. For literary-critical analysis see P. Weimar and E. Zenger, *Exodus*, Stuttgarter Bibelstudien 75, ²1979; for the structure of Ex. 5.1–6.1 as a composition, see U. Cassuto, *Exodus*, Jerusalem 1951 (Hebrew), 1967 (English), esp. 74f.

3. There are important comments on the psychology of the narrative and its constellations in L. Ragaz, *Die Bibel* 2, *Mose*, Zurich 1947, esp. 46f.; for the history of the political motives and ideas of the Exodus theme see M. Walzer, *Exodus and Revolution*, New York 1985.

4. Thus Weimar and Zenger, *Exodus* (n. 3).

5. The constellation is similar to that betweeen God and Satan in Rev. 12, see my *Apokalyse*, Einwürfe 2, Munich 1985, 5–61; esp. 48ff.

6. In the edition by A. Wünsche, *Bibliotheca Rabbinica*, Leipzig 1880–85, reprinted Hildesheim 1967, III, 66.

7. See also Ragaz, *Die Bibel* (n. 3), 55 (on Ex. 4.21).

8. Here Isaiah in particular should be remembered, since the hardening of the people was made his task; cf. G. Von Rad, *Old Testament Theology* II, London 1975, 151ff.; C. Hardmeier, 'Jesajas Verkündigungsabsicht und Jahwes Verstockungsauftrag in Jes. 6', in *FS H. W. Wolff*, Neukirchen 1981, 235–51; for hardening in Exodus see I. Willi-Plein, *Das Buch vom Auszug, 2. Mose*, Kleine Biblische Bibliothek, Neukirchen 1988, 35f., 47.

9. According to Wünsche, *Bibliotheca Rabbinica* (n. 6), 178f. (Midrash Shemot Rabba on Ex. 15.1).

10. Ibid., 170.

11. Whose strong hand is meant here? The answer to 'who is the subject?' should be the same as the answer to that question in the case of the hardening of Pharaoh's heart.

Does God Fail?

Theological considerations with a practical intent

Gotthard Fuchs

The very question which forms the title of this article must already seem rhetorical to those for whom God is long dead – either from exhaustion or erosion or because he has been murdered by human beings (the atheistic variant). Equally, the idea of the possible failure of God must seem obsolete to those for whom talk of a personal divine and diffuse religious feeling is enough (esoteric/neo-gnostic variants). However, for others the very question must seem blasphemous, obscene and godless. They take it for granted that God is the embodiment of life, truth, justice and power – the reality that determines and perfects all things. For this view, too – let us call it the theistic variant – the question is hardly legitimate, let alone settled or answered in the negative. That human beings, especially the other side of Eden, can and in fact must fail (?) – partially in some phases of their existence or even in the totality of their life – may be regarded as a brute fact of real history. But God? That human beings make others fail and reduce them to failure is similarly part of worldly existence as it is. But God? That everything must be done wherever possible to make such situations of failure *a priori* impossible or to cope with them later may be regarded as a commandment of practical reason, as a call of the *humanum* in us. But why involve God in this history? Why ask at all about the failure of God and charge God with failure? Is this not religious arrogance, indeed the ideologizing of human failure, even its theo-ontologizing? In this approach does not talk of God as God become a merely projective duplication of human need? Does this not ultimately lead to God becoming fully incorporated into the human community of need, at worst as an accomplice of human suffering?

However, we can put things the other way round. If human failing remained external to God, if God stood apathically beyond the histories of human suffering, then he could not truly be the redeeming and liberating

God. So the problem of theodicy is also involved in the question 'Can God fail?' Which God are we talking about, whether this God is being accepted or rejected? And if it is part of the reality of the true God also to be capable of failure, where is the opposition to him? In what does God fail?

One could regard such questions as superfluous games in the philosophy of religion and theology were it not that the humanity of men and women is always at stake in every thought of God, the question of what makes life successful for men and women both individually and socially, the future of human beings and the world. The theocentric focussing of the theme of failure intended here becomes fundamental above all if human beings see themselves faced with an ethical demand to avoid situations of failure wherever possible, or to master them creatively. Where does the motivation for this come from? Why should we take even the completely failed person, any person, seriously as a person? Why do we let ourselves be touched by the suffering of creation and by the 'tears of things'?

Any ethics, especially if it puts universal justice and solidarity programmatically at the centre, needs a religious and – from a Christian perspective – a theological foundation if it is not just to remain appellative and imperative, thus leading to the dilemma of merely heroic over-exertion. Therefore, first of all I shall make some comments on the context of the question in society (and the church) (I); then I shall develop their theological status systematically (II); finally I shall draw some practical and pastoral consequences (III). In so doing, for clarity of concepts, without developing a detailed phenomenology of failure here I shall keep to the image of the shipwreck: the situations will always be those of objective and subjective aporia, involving the development of resistance which is impossible to overcome (as a result of fate or through guilt), and the collapse of horizons of expectation and worlds of social and individual experience which have long provided support. Here I am referring to catastrophes of any kind, defeats on both a large and a small scale, the thwarting of initiatives and projects, collapses and mortal blows in personal and social relations, indications of competition with the character of partial or total finality.

I

There are reasons for asserting that in the modern world with a 'Western' stamp, the dominant model is that of the successful person, the victorious type in the competition of life, the first in career and competition, the invulnerable man (and of course in all these definitions one has to think in terms of the masculine sex). As Thomas Hobbes put it: 'But this race we must suppose to have no other goal, no other garland, but being foremost; and in it: To endeavour, is appetite. To be remiss, is sensuality. To consider them behind, is glory . . . Contunually to be out-gone is misery. Continually to out-go the next before us, felicity. And to forsake the course, is to die.'[1]

Certainly since then – not least since the famous Lisbon earthquake – there have been plenty of individual and social experiences of failure, of destruction, of crisis and defeat – some also as a result of nature, but almost always mediated through society and caused by *homo faber*. At no moment can there be any question of developing a scenario of the modern world in which the magnitude of the modern awareness of freedom and the results of Enlightenment, science and technology, are denounced. But the dialectic of progress and the Enlightenment (which are all too easily cited) have diagnostic value not only for the greatness but also for the misery of the modern world. Right down to everyday practice, the controlling norm of successful humanity is the ultimate victor in all the rivalries, the invulnerable Siegfried (whose weak point is concealed as much as possible, and the last window of whose vulnerability has to be closed by armament, no matter how much it costs). Following a pattern more or less of vitalism, indeed of social Darwinism, each person constantly wants more, and true life is defined in terms of the will to power, to having and to getting. The dominance of the stronger is taken as a social ideal. Depressions (whether economic, political or psychological) are regarded as commercial ac-cidents, are pigeon-holed as catastrophic setbacks, in a dynamic of progress which ultimately rushes on like a conveyor belt or a production line. (Calls for creative self-limitation, urgently made as a result of ecological crises and world-wide unfairness in distribution, are gaped at and mocked, like the prophecies of a Cassandra; plans to rethink alternative action remain the concern of a minority.)

As a consequence the poor (the impoverished!) person, the person who is economically and politically oppressed, but also the person handicapped by a neurosis or the complete failure, tends to be regarded as a minus, as an unperson or sub-person, as an omega figure, an anthropological zero. Where the producer is everything, the non-producer is nothing. In accordance with the destructive power of the 'all or nothing' ideal, in that case there are only winners and losers – and woe to the one who stands on the minus side, who goes into the red and constantly has to play the fatal zero-sum game. 'Man is a wolf to man' (Hobbes); 'man is God to man' (Feuerbach): the oppressed, the handicapped and the failures find themselves caught between such definitions of themselves, made by themselves and others, with the result that they are cast aside and regarded as rubbish.

Accordingly, history is the history of the victors, and the damned of this earth (like the damned parts of ourselves) can find no advocate or voice, far less real recognition or equal rights. Hence the sighing of creation, the suffering of endangered and destroyed nature, in us and around us. In the logic of modernity with its great increase in specialization, there is also an unholy division of work: the sick and the old, the 'crazy' and those who have incurred punishment, are isolated in special 'institutions' and split off in accordance with patterns of defensive delegation, so that incurably healthy, normal people can continue their triumphal progress undisturbed. Wherever failure, in whatever form, in fact shapes *all* human life and affects *everyone*, particular peoples, groups and individuals are made stigmatized bearers of symptoms, prototypes and representatives of failure, presumably the losing types *a priori*.

The modern victor anthropologies have also gained power in the churches, in sheer contradiction to their origin and function. Where the churches merely make themselves a moral institution, the task of which is to frame values, and where by delegation they allow themselves to be reduced to professional institutions for helping in accidents, they in fact help to maintain the ambivalence in the social system. Structurally they even run the risk of elevating to the religious dimension the schizoid division into winners and losers, and of legitimating it (e.g. through abstract theologies of guilt, suffering and sacrifice, or through merely 'caritative' concerns). The tendentious moralizing of the gospel of beatitudes on failures then leads, especially when associated with rigoristic and legalistic interpretations of Christianity, to a merely condescending 'treatment' of the marginalized in terms of looking after them, which at the same time reproduces and stabilizes prevailing victor anthropologies. The poor and the failures, who in the gospel are explicitly the preferential recipients of justice and are truly subjects, consequently become mere accident victims and disturbing special cases of the 'normal' blows of fate.

In this context it does not seem a coincidence that as far as I know there is at present no worked-out theological ethic of failure and that there is no specific pastoral theory of failure, despite the emphasis on a programme of 'coming of age' and participation. If failure is not already a basic element in the definition of human beings, of any human beings, then the very idea that God himself could fail must be irritating and alienating. If that is the case, it is vitally important to base situations of failure firmly at the centre of Christian belief in God. All ethics of solidarity, all pastoral theory of failure would ultimately remain voluntaristic and appellative if it were not grounded in the very mystery of God. The Christian imperative to perceive each person in his or her value and uniqueness, prior to and independently of their works, their successes and defeats, can only be realized (or seek to be realized) in a liberating way if it is grounded in the indicative of God's righteousness and is motivated and made effective by that. Universal solidarity, as a result of which all men and women in mutual need are equally winners and losers, i.e. subjects with finite freedom, can only be realized in believing participation and in accord with the action of the God who goes after the lost and failed and defines them anew in terms of the victims of history.

> Men go to God when they are sore bestead,
> Pray to him for succour, for his peace, for bread,
> For mercy for them sick, sinning, or dead,
> All men do so, Christian and unbelieving.[2]

II

Does God fail? This question is theologically meaningful only if there is no norm for conceiving of God which is taken as unalterable. Rather, the question prompts us once again to learn the Christian alphabet of the name of God and to investigate the genesis of the content and form of this confession of God. Is God a God who as the unmoved mover is apathically throned above the histories of human suffering? Is Spinoza's expedient valid, that as the embodiment of perfection God can neither love nor suffer, or, on the contrary, the view that human suffering is elevated into God himself, as it were affecting God in a quite personal way and thus 'changing' him? Which God is the true, the truly saving, God? God stands *in concreto* over against God, God against gods, God against idols. Is it a special mark of the true God that he bears the real possibility of failure within him, and thus makes himself truly capable of being touched and grasped? Only in a reciprocally and truly open history of God with human beings and of human beings with God can and must the question emerge whether this God cannot fail, and indeed does not fail, again and again – with human beings, with his people, with creation, with the world, and thus ultimately in himself and his project? In this connection some recollections of the Bible and assertions from systematic theology may be noted in respect of the history of the Christian discovery of God (which of course cannot be separated from that of Judaism, though it is to be distinguished from it).

As is well known, the gospel of the Old and New Testaments as it were emerges and proves itself from three basic crisis situations: exodus, exile and crucifixion. The bibliodrama of the history of this God with human beings or, more precisely, with his people and, progressively, in a more complicated way with individuals in it, proves to be the way by which God's divinity reveals itself increasingly clearly in humanity, in the danger to his people. In the very situations of failure and defeat this God proves to be utterly reliable and liberating – creating victory in defeat, calling being out of nothingness, life out of death. When his people are in danger, this

God puts himself at risk, in a real covenant partnership which he makes possible. From this perspective the whole Bible can be read as a document of creative mourning, a testimony to the assimilation of the history (or histories) of failure in faith against the horizon of the ever more reliable God. It is as if the load-bearing capacity of the covenant between this God and his people in favour of the world as a whole had to be tested and proved to the uttermost, so that in principle no human situation can ever be godless, and the most abysmal defeats, the worst experiences of exile, the most depressing invasions are situations in which God's faithfulness and godliness are manifested. 'God seeks what has disappeared' (Koheleth 3.15). That this God, with a particular name and a concrete history, is really the 'lover of life' (Wisdom 11.23), who does not want human death and failure, must be proved and tested in situations of extreme threat – with all the power of resistance and hoping against all hope, without any security, but with increasing confidence.

The loyalty of this God – in contrast to the gods – becomes dramatically credible precisely where, in anthropomorphic terms, the whole breadth of human feelings and modes of behaviour is asserted in God. YHWH himself is the one whose heart is rent, who is torn between anger and lamentation, rage and sorrow, and who finally in repentance recalls his promises to his people and will not depart from his voluntary commitment to human beings and the world (Hosea 11). It is YHWH who laments *with* his people, but at the same time laments *over* his people and accuses them. God's power to support the world which he has created and the people whom he has elected – serving as a representative of the nations – shows itself at its most shattering in his patience, in the withholding of his anger, which primarily leaves time for repentance and keeps real history open. Hearing the misery of his people which cries to heaven, and identifying himself with the suffering righteous, full of empathy for man and beast (Jonah 4.10), this God allows himself to be drawn into compassion, affected through and through. The prophets of Israel give an insight, often in real symbolic identification, into the theodramatics of this history of the covenant. Thus, for example, Jeremiah and Ezekiel can say that God leaves his temple – disappointed, angry, having utterly failed (cf. Isa. 7; Ezek. 11.6). Here such anthropomorphic talk of the reality of God is in no way external to this reality, but creates and discloses it.

Jesus stands out in a special way in this open and committed history of God with his people. Acting on the basis of a unique certainty of God, the prophet and wisdom teacher of Nazareth turns specifically to those who are failing and have failed – with the claim that it is in so doing that he corresponds to God himself and God's love of the world. In the specific weakness of Jesus (and God) for his fellow men and women who fail, God's power is brought to bear and to bring about change. Because the power of Jesus does not answer violence with counter-violence, but makes itself vulnerable in the extreme, Jesus himself ultimately becomes the failure *par excellence*, the crucified one, the one who is stigmatized. Here Jesus fails, here God fails – over the powers of violence, anxiety and lying among men and women. But *in* the failure of Jesus, *in* the cross of Jesus – and in no way by-passing them – there is proof of the omnipotence of impotent love, of God's loyalty and reliability. So it may now paradoxically be asserted that God does not fail in this failed man. As the New Testament writings show throughout, the Christianing Easter confession in no way stills the questing movement between God and humankind, but discloses it in an explosive way. In the drama on the cross, involving God's non-violence and human acts of violence, we can see how far this God himself embodies love of enemies, is inwardly touched and affected by the suffering of the just, by the failing of creation. The whole history of faith up to the present has accentuated this theodramatic of the covenant between God and man in a variety of ways, in teaching and in life, in dogma and liturgy: what has ultimately proved successful in the failed God-man is constantly at risk again, the covenant between God and the world. *In* situations of defeat and failure, undergoing these, he claims that he is the faithful God.

While noting that theological statements relate to a relationship of a special kind, to a particular communicative proaxis, to sum up with we can maintain that, in consistently historical terms, the real possibility of failure is part of the mystery of the loyalty of God himself. To this degree he has involved himself with human beings and the world, making himself free and binding himself in freedom. God's love of the world implies suffering. 'What kind of suffering is it that he suffered for us? The suffering is love'[3] – or more accurately, love of enemies. Specifically, the love of God, as the history of humanity, the history of Israel and the history of the church show, has always partly failed. 'My people, my people, what have I done to you, how have I troubled you? Answer me,' goes the Good Friday liturgy.

That the real possibility of the total failure of God in free men and women and the world cannot (or can no longer) become real is the mystery of God in Jesus and of Jesus in God. Here is one who has wholly accepted the distress of God in the world and has given a creative answer in freedom. Now both these things have become manifest in Jesus Christ. Classical christology has worked this out in the doctrine of the *communicatio idiomatum*: God's unconditioned and ultimately victorious reliability in the midst of failure. There is a bond between God and humankind even in failure. God and man have eternally become one with each other, unmixed and undivided: God's need is human salvation; human salvation is God's victory. It is God's will wholly to be in need of human beings, and it is the greatness of humankind to dare to want to be acceptable to God. From now on in the Holy Spirit, both these things are made possible: here is God's power in human weakness, God's asking and the human response, human failure in God's all-supporting and compassionate reliability. 'He who was rich became poor for your sake, to make you rich through his poverty(!)' (II Cor. 8.9).

There may be, may have to be, christological talk in this sense of the God who suffers and fails, but in it a precise distinction needs to be made: God does not suffer in order as it were simply to be able to come to himself in others, as was sometimes thought in German Idealism. Rather, God's suffering derives exclusively from his freedom and love. Here, descending and being brought low, he seeks to take part in human failure, changing it and redeeming it (this marks the origin and significance of the Christian doctrine of the Trinity). A God who became himself only by going through world history would be merely a projection of human beings in search of themselves. However, the God who does not need human beings, but wills to be in need of them and makes the omnipotence of his love concrete in its extreme impotence to the extreme, at the same time reveals that human beings are ultimately far more than their works, than their victories or defeats. Those who believe in this God and thus see themselves justified as human beings, cease to be anxious about themselves and become free to be anxious about God in the world, to be capable of taking up God's cause and really helping him in the power of the Spirit of Jesus (as, for example, among the great mystics).

> Men go to God when he is sore bestead,
> Find him poor and scorned, without shelter or bread,
> Whelmed under weight of the wicked, the weak, the dead;
> Christians stand by God in his hour of grieving.[4]

III

Christian ethics and pastoral work can be defined as Christian – and that is all that we are concerned with here – only if it is realized that they are a response, made possible by the Spirit, of human action to God's presence. The imperative need to avoid injustice, not to allow fellow human beings and creation to fail, and to support them creatively in failure, is based solely on the initiative of God's love of the world. That human beings are more than what they do and what they do not do, that their happiness and failure, their successes and failures, are steeped in the compassion of the God who is omnipotent in his powerlessness – that alone is the basis for going after those who fail, with God and helping God, and perceiving them as subjects before God and their fellow men and women precisely in their failure. Only to the degree that Christian faith is realized as an authentic relationship in which the characteristic of this God is seen to be the way in which he shares suffering, do courage and humility grow, so that the failures of human beings beyond Eden are seen to be as human, as normal, as their successes. Where unbelievers are always at least in in danger of giving way to their 'natural' anxieties and 'natural' abhorrence of failure and those who have failed to the point of humiliating or suppressing them, those who in faith share in God's suffering with us gain freedom for real solidarity and comunion with all, particularly the poor, the hungry and those in need. Furthermore, they see God's own need in them and seek to alleviate it (cf. Matt. 25).

This gives rise to the imperative need strictly to repudiate and to fight against any form of fetishizing failure, any theontologizing of defeat, any ideologizing transfiguration of suffering in and for itself. But it is no less important to avoid any form of trivialization which spares and suppresses suffering. 'The logic of failure' in the vicious circle of the will-to-power driven by anxiety needs to be bold in analysing the causes and consequences of this will-to-power and in distinguishing between agents and victims. According to a depth-psychological hermeneutic of Christian belief in God, what is needed is to work creatively and communally through the whole arsenals of defence and transference in order to overcome the pernicious division into winners and losers, victors and victims. An essential supplement to this is the need of an analysis, in terms of a political hermeneutic of faith, of the vicious circles in society as a result of which so many people fail and make others fail. If there was a need, in connection with the reality of God, to do justice to anthropomorphic talk, so here the theomorphic nature of human histories of suffering needs to be stressed. The work of recollection and mourning, of lament and accusation, of suffering together out of love and solidarity (not out of masochism!), are accordingly central basic attitudes of believers – in accordance with God's own attitude. Without any certainty that failure may not be the last word of history in detail and as a whole, this attitude nevertheless cherishes the deepest certainty of hope that God will ultimately be all in all to world and humankind.

It seems important both for the individual's biography of faith and for ecclesiogenesis to take very careful note of the particular stages in the maturing of a Christian. To bid farewell to a God thought to be omnipotent, to whom a still infantile belief in God would correspond, and in closer discipleship of Jesus also to recognize in his distress the God who fails and has needs, presupposes a long process of growth. The more deeply believers are bound to this God and called by him, the more vulnerable and more disturbed they will become, shaped to the same degree by relaxation and passion, and as it were wounded by compassionate concern for God's success in the world. The example of many mystics through history and at the present day displays something of this aim of Christian incarnation. Failure and success are lived out and proved in abysmal unity, in the dark night of the senses and the spirit. The more men and women are thus concerned for God, the more they can be selflessly concerned for this world, acting and suffering, standing by God in his need.

> God goes to every man when sore bestead,
> Feeds body and spirit with his bread;
> For Christians, pagans alike he hangs dead,
> and both alike forgiving.[5]

Translated by John Bowden

Bibliography

I would like to mention at least the following titles as a background to my comments:

Ulrich Mauser, *Gottesbild und Menschenwerdung. Eine Untersuchung zur Einheit des Alten und Neuen Testaments*, Tübingen 1971; Hans Urs von Balthasar, *Theodramatik I–III*, Einsiedeln 1978ff.; Jürgen Moltmann, *The Trinity and the Kingdom of God*, London and New York 1981; Dietrich Dörner, *Die Logik des Misslingens. Strategisches Denken in komplexen Situationen*, Reinbek bei Hamburg 1988; Friedrich Wilhelm Marquardt et al. (eds.), *Umgang mit Niederlagen*, Einwürfe 5, Munich 1988; Thomas Pröpper, *Erlösungsglaube und Freiheitsgeschichte. Eine Skizze zur Soteriologie*, Munich 1988; Willi Oelmüller (ed.), *Theo Dizee*, Paderborn 1990; Peter Kuhn, *Gottes Trauer und Klage in der rabbinischer Überlieferung, Talmud und Midrasch*, Leiden 1978; Hans Jonas, *Gott nach Auschwitz*, Frankfurt 1986.

Notes

1. Thomas Hobbes, *The Elements of Law Natural and Politic*, London 1969, 47f.
2. Dietrich Bonhoeffer, *Letters and Papers from Prison*, The Enlarged Edition, London and New York 1971, p. 348.
3. Origen, *Homily VI in Ezechielem*, PG 13, 714f.
4. See n. 2.
5. Ibid.

Contributors

NORBERT GREINACHER was born in 1931 in Freiburg im Breisgau. He studied at Freiburg im Breisgau, Paris and Vienna, gained his doctorate in 1955 and was ordained priest in 1956. He has been Professor of Practical Theology at the Catholic Faculty of the University of Tübingen since 1969. His publications include: *Soziologie der Pfarrei*, Freiburg 1955; *Die Kirche in der städtischen Gesellschaft*, Mainz 1966; *Einführung in die Praktische Theologie*, Munich 1976; *Gelassene Leidenschaft*, Zurich 1977; *Gemeindepraxis. Analysen und Aufgaben*, Munich 1979; *Der Fall Küng. Eine Dokumentation*, Munich 1980; *Freiheitsrechte für Christen?*, Munich 1980; *Christsein als Beruf*, Zurich 1981; *Im Angesicht meiner Feinde – Mahl des Friedens*, Gütersloh 1982; *El Salvador – Massaker im Namen der Freiheit*, Hamburg 1982; *Der Konflikt um die Theologie der Befreiung*, Zurich 1985; *Kirche der Armen. Zur Theologie der Befreiung*, Munich³ 1985; *Umkehr und Neubeginn*, Fribourg CH 1986; *Menschlich Leben*, Zurich 1986; *Der Schrei nach Gerechtigkeit*, Munich 1986.

J. MARK THOMAS gained his PhD at the University of Chicago and works as a senior research fellow for the Au Sable Institute of Environmental Studies of Mancelona, Michigan. His recent works include editing and introducing Paul Tillich, *The Spiritual Situation in our Technical Society*, Macon, Georgia 1988; *Ethics and Technoculture*, Lanham, Maryland 1987.

ALOIS MÜLLER was born in 1945 in Ruswil/Lucerne. He studied theology in Lucerne and Freiburg im Breisgau and at the Institut Catholique in Lyons, where he received his licentiate. He did further study of philosophy and German in the University of Zurich, where he also worked as an academic assistant. He teaches philosophy and social ethics in secondary schools and at the Evangelische Gemeinschaft of the two High Schools in Zurich. His publications include *Religion des Bürgers. Zivilreligion in Amerika und Europa*, Munich 1986 (with H. Kleger).

KARL-JOSEF KUSCHEL was born in 1948. He studied German and theology at the universities of Bochum and Tübingen. He did his doctoral studies in Tübingen, where he was an academic assistant, and from 1981 has worked at the Institute for Ecumenical Research and Catholic Faculty there. He qualified as a university teacher in 1989. As well as editing many works, he has written *Jesus in der deutschsprächigen Gegenwartsliteratur* (1978): *Heute noch knien? Über ein Bild von Edouard Manet* (1979); *Stellvertreter Christi? Der Papst in der zeitgenössischen Literatur* (1980); *Gottesbilder-Menschenbilder. Blicke durch die Literatur unserer Zeit* (1985): *Weil wir uns auf dieser Erde nicht ganz zu Hause fühlen. Zwölf Schriftsteller über Religion und Literatur* (1985); *Geboren vor aller Zeit? Der Streit um Christi Ursprung* (1990).

DIETMAR MIETH was born in 1940. After studying theology, German and philosophy he gained a doctorate in theology at Würzburg in 1968 and qualified as a university teacher in theological ethics at Tübingen in 1974; in 1974 he became Professor of Moral Theology in Fribourg, Switzerland and since 1981 has been Professor of Theological Ethics in Tübingen. His publications include *Die Einheit von* vita activa *und* vita contemplativa, Regensburg 1969; *Dichtung, Glaube und Moral*, Mainz 1976; *Epik und Ethik*, Tübingen 1976; *Moral und Erfahrung*. Fribourg CH and Freiburg im Breisgau ³1983; *Gotteserfahrung-Weltverantwortung*, Munich 1982; *Die neuen Tugenden*, Düsseldorf 1984; *Ehe als Entwurf*, Mainz 1984; *Arbeit und Menschenwürde*, Freiburg im Breisgau 1985; *Die Spannungseinheit von Theorie und Praxis*, Fribourg CH – Freiburg im Breisgau 1986.

ERIKA SCHUCHARDT was born in Hamburg in 1940 and is a professor in the University of Hannover. After studying social sciences, special teaching and adult education, she taught in high schools and special schools until 1970, and then became head of the division of pedagogy, psychology and philosophy at the Volkshochschule Hannover until 1975, then going on to lecture at the University of Hannover. Of her many publications, *Why is this happening to me? Guidance and hope for those who suffer*, Minneapolis 1990, was awarded the German Literature Prize.

CARMEN PÉREZ (María del Carmen Pérez Babot-Fernández) was born in Barcelona, Spain, in 1959 but has lived in Peru since she was four. She studied psychology in the University of San Agustin de Arequipa in Peru and some philology in Barcelona. Since 1978 she has been a social promoter and pastoral worker in Ilo and El Agustino, a poor area of Lima.

She is a full-time editor on the journals *Páginas* and *Signos*, published by the Centro de Estudos y Publicaciones and the Centro Bartolomé de las Casas, and also works for a popular education organization run by the Jesuits.

NAZAIRE BITOTO ABENG was born in Cameroun in 1946. After studies in Cameroun and Paris and doctoral work in Münster with Professor Metz, in 1986 he took up work on the staff of the Missionswissenschaftlicher Institut Missio e.V. in Aachen. He is joint editor of the bibliography *Theologie im Kontext*. His dissertation was published under the title *Von der Freiheit zur Befreiung: Die Kirchen- und Kolonialgeschichte Kameruns*, Berne and Frankfurt am Main 1989. His article 'An Interpretation of the Lord's Prayer in the African Context', *Misereor*, Verlag Aachen, 1988, 8f., has appeared in several languages, and he has also written two articles, 'Afrikanisches Christsein in Kirche und Gesellschaft' and 'Jesus Christus als Proto-Ahn. Der afrikanische Weg zum Vater', both in *Ordensnachrichten Wien* 29.5, 1989, 47–58, 58–65.

ELISABETH BLESKE studied German and theology at the University of Münster and then did her doctorate in moral theology. After training in communications therapy and as a marriage counsellor she taught in schools and then became an adviser in moral theology at the University of Munich. She now works training marriage counsellors in the Institute for Research and Training in Communications Therapy in Munich. As well as numerous articles on marriage, marriage counselling and related fields she has written *Konfliktfeld Ehe und christliche Ethik*, Munich 1981.

JÜRGEN EBACH was born in 1945 in Kirchen/Sieg. After studying protestant Theology and Oriental Studies, he became lecturer and professor in Bochum and since 1983 has been Professor of Biblical Exegesis and Theology at the University of Paderborn. His publications include *Kritik und Utopie (Ez. 40–48)*, 1972; *Weltentstehung und Kulturentwicklung bei Philo von Byblos*, 1979; *Das Erbe der Gewalt*, 1980; *Leviathan und Behemoth*, 1984; *Ursprung und Ziel*, 1986; *Kassandra und Jona*, 1987; *Theologische Reden, mit denen man keinen Staat machen kann*, 1989; with H. -E. Bahr, K. Raiser and K. Wengst he produced a volume *Umgang mit Niederlagen*, Einwürfe 5, Munich 1988, which is also relevant to the theme of failure. He has also written many articles.

GOTTHARD FUCHS was born in 1938 in Halle/S. After studying philosophy and Catholic theology he was ordained priest in Paderborn in 1963; he has long been active in pastoral work and counselling and in the theological faculties of Münster and Bamberg. Since 1983 he has been Director of the Rabanus Maurus Catholic Academy of the Dioceses of Fulda, Limburg and Mainz. His publications include *Glaube als Widerstandskraft*, Frankfurt 1986; *Mensch und Natur. Auf der Suche nach der Verlorenen Einheit*, Frankfurt 1989; *Die dunkle Nacht der Sinne. Leiderfahrung und christliche Mystik*, Düsseldorf 1989, and many articles on theology and spirituality.

Members of the Advisory Committee for Practical Theology

Directors

Norbert Greinacher	Tübingen	West Germany
Norbert Mette	Münster	West Germany

Members

Carlos Abaitua	Vitoria	Spain
Rosemary Crumlin RSM	Victoria	Australia
Virgil Elizondo	San Antonio, Texas	USA
Segundo Galilea	Santiago	Chile
Alfonso Gregory	Rio de Janeiro	Brazil
Frans Haarsma	Nijmegen	Netherlands
Adrian Hastings	Leeds	England
François Houtart	Louvain-la-Neuve	Belgium
Jan Kerkhofs SJ	Louvain-Heverlee	Belgium
Hubert Lepargneur OP	São Paulo	Brazil
Anthony Lobo SJ	Washington DC	USA
Angelo Macchi SJ	Milan	Italy
Alois Müller	Lucern	Switzerland
Thomas Nyiri	Budapest	Hungary
Emile Pin	Poughkeepsie, NY	USA
†Karl Rahner SJ	Innsbruck	Austria
Rosemary Radford Ruether	Evanston, Ill	USA
Sidbe Semporé	Cotonou	Republic of Benin
Francisco Soto	Jalapa, Veracruz	Mexico
Yorick Spiegel	Frankfurt am Main	West Germany
Wevitavidanelage Don Sylvester	Galle	Sri Lanka
Rolf Zerfass	Höchberg	West Germany

Members of the Board of Directors